THIS IS
THAT

TRAVEL GUIDE TO CANADA

D0950389

"As the famous Canadian once
said, Canada is best when read."
ANOTHER FAMOUS CANADIAN

THIS IS
THAT

TRAVEL GUIDE TO CANADA

Published by The Tite Group
219 Dufferin St
Toronto ON M6K 3J1
www.thetitegroup.com

Cataloguing data available from Library and Archives Canada
ISBN 978-0-9952589-0-7 (paperback)
ISBN 978-0-9952589-1-4 (ebook)

Produced by Page Two
www.pagetwostrategies.com
Cover and interior design by Peter Cocking
Printed and bound in Canada by Friesens

PHOTO CREDITS:
Shutterstock: 6, 28, 46, 55, 59, 65, 66, 75,
84, 90, 108 (top), 113, 114, 130, 133, 138

iStock: 12, 14, 23, 27, 31, 32, 35, 36, 38, 39, 40, 42, 48, 52,
54, 56, 58, 60, 62, 69, 70, 77, 79, 80, 81, 82, 87, 88, 93,
94, 97, 98, 101, 104, 105, 106, 107, 108 (bottom),
109, 111, 116, 119, 123, 124, 126, 128, 131, 135, 137, 140

Peter Cocking: pp 19, 100

16 17 18 19 20   5 4 3 2 1

No part of this work is meant to be taken seriously.
Photocopying this book would be a pain in the butt, so don't
do it. Reading this book out loud on a family road trip is strongly
recommended and in some provinces is law. No vowels
were harmed in the writing of this book. Our lawyers
have read the book and think it's "somewhat amusing."
Legally speaking, that's a compliment.

Contents

Foreword

BY **DAVE THOMAS**

N OT SINCE JOHN MURRAY began publishing *Murray's Handbooks for Travellers* in London in 1836 has a more definitive travel guide been written. Even Eugene Fodor's famous travel guides launched after World War II pale in comparison to this newest entry into the travel guide compendium—*This is That: Travel Guide to Canada*.

It is expertly penned by Canadians whose travels across Canada for their famous radio show, *This is That*, made them experts on everything Canadian, from Bonavista to Vancouver Island and from the Arctic Circle to the Great Lakes' waters. Of course I'm referring to *This is That* uber hosts, Pat Kelly and Peter Oldring, who also happen to be documentarians, journalists, and itinerant rovers of the Great White North.

Like Robert Louis Stevenson, these intellectual vagabonds travel "not to go anywhere, but to go, travelling for travel's sake." Their destinations are never a place, but a new way of seeing things. Because, as Peter put it so aptly while sipping the signature Northwest Collins at the Q Bar at the Empress Hotel in Victoria, "a traveller without observation is a bird without wings."

His partner, Pat, chuckled and added, "It's the journey, not the arrival time that matters. A journey is best measured in friends, not miles."

"Indeed," added Peter, "a wise traveller never needs to leave his own country because he knows he can travel the world in search of meaning only to return home to find it."

Pat ordered another Collins and wistfully offered this rejoinder: "A ship in harbour is safe, but that's not why ships were built. You see, travel makes a wise man wiser and a fool only more of an ass."

Peter smiled, a knowing smile, as he took another long pull from his straw. "I think the traveller sees what he sees. The tourist sees what he has come to see."

Refining that thought even more, Pat added, "The real voyage of discovery across this great land consists not in seeking new landscapes, but in having new eyes."

And so it went, long into the night, as these Canadian knights of the road shared epithets of wisdom with me over many more Canadian Collins and then on through multiple doubles of the finest Scotch, finally capping it all off with splashes of Grand Marnier over ice. We closed the Q Bar of the Empress Hotel that night but continued singing and laughing in the lobby until hotel security kindly offered to escort us to our suites. Clearly, these gentlemen were such fans of *This is That* that no courtesy offered to these radio giants would be withheld from their humble guest.

> "The real voyage of discovery across this great land consists not in seeking new landscapes, but in having new eyes."

I left Victoria the next day, confident that writing a prologue for these two pathfinders of all things Canada was not only my obligation as their friend, but an extreme honour because they are, without doubt, the self-proclaimed Fodors of the new millennium. This book is their endowment to Canadian readers, in fact all readers, everywhere. Embrace it as the priceless hereditament that it is. Savour its pages with the full knowledge that these nomadic wanderers are taking you on an amazing journey while you sit, safely at home in your armchair or wherever you enjoy non-fiction at its best. It's a virtual journey that will leave you with a love and an understanding of your country that few are ever privileged to enjoy. For my part, I consider myself fortunate to be their friend and a proud Canadian.

Dave Thomas
Malibu, California

DAVE THOMAS is a Canadian comedian, actor, and television writer. He is best known for portraying Doug McKenzie on *SCTV,* as well as in the film *Strange Brew.* He has the distinct honour of being the only Canadian to swim in all 40,000 of the country's lakes.

Introduction

CONGRATULATIONS! BY opening this book you have made the decision to travel Canada! What great news!

Since 2010, *This Is That* has been telling stories on CBC Radio about the people and places that make up this unbelievable country. Which is why we felt it was our national responsibility to share with the world our deep knowledge and unabashed passion for this great land that we not only call home, but have reported on so accurately over the years.

From Tofino to Twillingate, Canada is chock full of places. In fact, according to the latest census, Canada has over one trillion places, including cities, towns, brooks, sounds, nooks, crannies, gullies, gulfs, wharfs, islands, inlets, peninsulas, piazzas, promenades, coves, caves, cliffs, graves, bluffs, burghs, burrows, burbs, forests, foreclosures, fortresses, lakes, and malls.

So whether it's pleasure or leisure that brings you to Canada, let us be your dependable travel companions as you discover the majesty of what the Internet calls "One of North America's Top Three Must-Visit Nations."

This guide aims to help those unaccustomed to life in Canada. From how we move our bodies in an athletic sense to how we move our bodies in a transportation sense; from how we like to match our tattoos with our personalized licence plates to how we pronounce the word "smoothie"—this book will have you feeling like an "oyster trapper" (regional slang for *local resident*) or a "potash pugger" (more regional slang for *local resident*) in no time.

TESTIMONIAL

"They don't got anything that Minnesota don't."

LADY FROM MINNESOTA

In writing this guide we never took for granted the great responsibility that comes with holding someone's vacation in the palm of our hands. We set out to write the most thorough, comprehensive, and accurate travel guide ever published about Canada. After reading this book, we believe you'll agree—we tried.

From all of us at *This Is That*, *thank you* for buying this book, *please* enjoy it, and finally, *sorry* (we're contractually obligated to apologize in this introduction). It is our true hope that you will read this book, share it, then deliver it to its final resting place at a summer cabin or cottage outhouse, where it can be enjoyed by generations to come.

So with that, don't just stand there ... Canada awaits!*

---

* When in doubt, the Wi-Fi password is always: ohcanada1967

WEATHER TRANSPORTATION

ESSENTIALS

CUSTOMS BAGGAGE

AND

EMERGENCIES CURRENCY

BASICS

POLITICS HISTORY

What Is Canada?

CLASSIFIED BY THE rest of the world as a country, Canada stretches from the U.S. in the south to the Ice Pole in the north. Surrounded by almost all of the world's oceans, it has long been considered "ye olde top hat" of the isle of North America.

Canada is divided into four distinct regions: Over There, Down There, Up There, and Nowhere. Visitors to Canada will often think they are Nowhere when in fact they may be Over There or, more likely, Up There. Each region looks and feels different, with its own style of architecture, its own characteristic foods, and its own type of swearing.

Although Canada is filled with vibrant cities, including the metropoli of Hamilton, Regina, St. Albert, Drummondville, and Duncan, it is predominantly a rural country. The influence of "the land" echoes throughout Canadian culture, revealing itself in national legislation which requires every citizen own boots. Perhaps the most astonishing feature of the country is its obscene amount of vast space. From huge tracts of undeveloped land littered with interminable trees to unfathomable expanses with nothing in sight, Canada is an agoraphobic's worst nightmare.

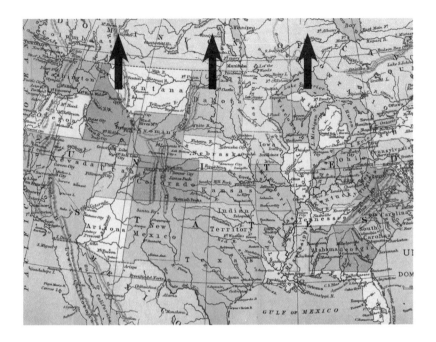

Research indicates that Ottawa is the official capital of Canada, but most residents use Baker Lake, Nunavut—the exact centre of the country—as their primary place of congregation.

In all this vastness, there are endless types of trips to take in Canada: you could visit a city, a region, a river, a drive-through, or a 50-year-old church.

Why Are You Coming?

Before coming to Canada, it is important to ask yourself what you want to get from the visit. It's also important that you have an exit strategy. Many visitors wooed by Canada's charms have found it next to impossible to leave.

If you ask the average Canadian why you should visit Canada, they'd likely say, "I dunno. The only thing I'd wanna do is maybe go skiing? Niagara Falls? Or maybe take the train from Banff to Vancouver?"

If you're looking to take a romantic trip, consider France. It's full of spots for kissing. Got kids? There are a dozen Disney parks around the world, and none of them are in Canada. If you want fun in the sun, Canada has beaches, but they're not *beach* beaches.

Sometimes you see a person win a trip to Canada on *Wheel of Fortune,* and they kinda shrug and say, "I guess." That's what your reaction to the country will be if you don't make sure you know what you want from your trip.

The Best Time to Visit

There is positively no reason to visit Canada during the winter months. *Canadians* don't even visit one another then. This means that as a visitor, your travel period is limited to the month of summer.

Beyond that, the single most important factor in deciding when to visit Canada is the bug schedule. It's crucial to recognize that, for three weeks, the entire country is ravaged by either mosquitoes or blackflies. Some have even told of an insect with the face of a hornet and the body of a domesticated turkey. This makes the ideal window for a trip somewhere between July 28th and August 9th.

TESTIMONIAL

"I was surprised to find out it was a real country, with real things to do."

AN AMERICAN TRAVELLER

Be warned: This is also when Canadians take their holidays. Although the country does not close down entirely during this period, a general apathy sets in and a laissez-faire cloud hangs over all regions. If you stick to this time frame, however, weather conditions should be ideal, except in the city of Toronto, where merciless heat and humidity can drive you into madness.

Getting There

Whether you are travelling by air, sea, rail, or road, prices increasingly depend on which of the travel websites owned by the same company you use. Most discount sites offer great fares, but after taxes and surcharges are added, you can expect to pay full price.

• By Air

Canada's airports are a cinch to navigate. It's as easy as landing in YYJ, transferring to YYG, and getting a connecting flight through YYC, then landing in YYZ. If you end up in YEG, YVR, YUL, YGE, YOF, or YIK, a local airport representative should be able to tell you why (or Y).

• By Bus

Without question, the bus is the best way to get to Canada. Buses in U.S. border towns offer affordable rates, onboard unisex washroom, and unnerving amounts of eye contact. Plus you meet the most interesting people on the bus, like Ron. He's starting his life over in Canada but will probably be the reason everyone on the bus gets searched.

TESTIMONIAL

"We quite enjoyed the really flat part in the middle of the country. Watching our dog run away for miles was a thrill."

KING LUIS OF SPAIN

• By Train

The railroad played a key part in forming the country, so it makes sense that you can affordably travel with ease by train in Canada. High-speed rail, however, is pretty much nonexistent. And the low-speed trains constantly have to stop when they run into cows. Still, it's pretty romantic, considering the cost of a train trip is four times that of a flight.

Weather by Region

	OVER THERE	DOWN THERE	UP THERE	NOWHERE
January	Rainy	Cold	Cold	Cold
February	Cold	Cold	Brutal	Brutal
March	T-shirt Weather	Cold	Cold	Cold
April	Sorta Cold	Sorta Cold	Sorta Cold	Sorta Cold
May	Cold Again	Cold Again	Cold Again	Cold Again
June	Kinda Warm	Kinda Warm	Kinda Warm	Kinda Warm
July	Actually Nice	Actually Nice	Actually Nice	Actually Nice
August	Too Hot	Gross	Unbearable	Too Hot
September	Won't Make Up Its Mind	Colder Than It Looks	Sorta Warm	It's Crazy Out There
October	Sweater Weather	Sweater Weather	Sweater Weather	Sweater Weather
November	Soup Weather	Chowder Weather	Stew Weather	Chili Weather
December	Warmest Christmas Ever	Cold	Cold	Stupid Cold

- **By Ferry**

Though slower than travelling by plane, the ferries from Britain and Japan offer the cheapest means of travelling to Canada. The length of the trip can vary, but travellers should set aside at least 120 hours. If you are planning on making passage in the cargo hold of a larger ferry, you need to pack food, water, and an empty jug for waste.

- **By Car**

Canada and the USA share the longest unprotected border in the world. The border checkpoints are usually clogged with Canadians who have made day trips to buy VCRs and jeans. To avoid the wait, cross in the winter on one of the many frozen lakes between Minnesota and Manitoba. Also, as a general note to American motorists, no need to waste time plotting your journey with a map—there is a simple rule of thumb: Drive north until you have to turn off the A/C and roll up the windows.

Travel Tip

Going through airport security is a breeze if you remember this simple mnemonic device: B4B&B4BBBBBD0 ("Bins for bags and bins for belts but bottles better be disposed of").

If you act suspiciously, guards tend to be a bit prickly and will make you feel like a toddler who has just broken one of Granny's vases. If you act courteously and respectfully, the guards tend to be a bit prickly and will make you feel like a toddler who has just broken one of Granny's vases. No matter how rude and ornery the guards are, give them a break because *you're* the one going on holiday.

So if you want to join me for a while
Just grab your hat, come travel light—that's hobo style.
Maybe tomorrow, I'll want to settle down,
Until tomorrow, I'll just keep moving on.
EARLY CANADIAN HYMN

From Customs to Customs

There are two types of customs in Canada: the Customs you have to go through and the customs you have to perform.

- **Canadian Customs**

Canadian Customs agents are multilingual, polite, and genuinely interested in where you come from. They also seem to have a keen interest in what's in your bag. They are the kind of people you might consider dating, but they're not marriage material because ultimately you're just too different.

- **Canadian Customs Customs**

When going through Canadian Customs, it's customary for ladies to curtsy, men to tip their hats, and children to perform the "I'm a little teapot" dance. In turn, it's customary for the border guard to offer a selection of biscuits representing the history of Canada. If the biscuits are refused, a tax is levied for each member of the travelling party. Kisses on the cheek are then offered thrice to the eldest member of the party. Simple.

What to Bring

- **Baggage**

When you're starting a relationship, baggage is the last thing you want, but when you start travelling, it's the first thing. Make sure you bring a bag that has plenty of room on the inside and even more on the outside. Because remember: The whole world is just what's happening outside your suitcase.

||||||||||||||||||||||||||||||||||||||||||||||||||||||||||||||||||||||||||||||||||||||||||||||||||
THREE ESSENTIAL BAGS FOR TRAVEL IN CANADA

The Fanny Pack
If you don't want to look like a tourist, bring a fanny pack. All Canadian men wear fanny packs around their ample hips. It's what gives Canadian men their famous sexy silhouette. Fanny packs are also great for holding lip balms and coupons.

The Clutch
What do classy women from Saskatoon to Moncton have in common? They all carry clutches. The clutch is a must-have accessory that elevates any outfit. Picture yourself strolling down the Kamloops Riviera, carrying a clutch full of a third of the junk you normally carry in your purse.

Travel Tip
It's smart to bring enough clean underwear to last your entire trip because, while washing machines are common, it's nearly impossible to calculate a metric load of laundry.

The Duffel Bag
Kirk Duffel was born in Edmonton, where, after growing tired of more refined luggage, he invented the duffel bag. He wanted a bag that screamed, "I got this for free!" This is also the go-to bag for any mysterious drifter who has to leave town in the middle of the night.

||||||||||||||||||||||||||||||||||||||||||||||||||||||||||||||||||||||||||||||||||||||||||||||||||

• Clothes
Canada is not a nude country. In fact, during the winter months, most Canadians are covered from head to toe, exposing only their eyes, nose, and mouth. This is one of the factors that keeps Canada's population size in check. In summertime, Canadians wear

A typical stance when looking at Canada

"Lake Clothes." It's not hard to follow the dress code in order to fit in with your Canadian hosts. Shorts vary from two to four cargo pockets. T-shirts are obtained as a result of participating in a fun run. Footwear consists of sturdy walking shoes or sandals.

- **Travel Documents**
  For most visitors, a passport is all that is needed to visit Canada. If you don't have a passport, you may use a letter from your head of state or a utility bill.

Travel Tip

The *This is That: Travel Guide to Canada* is required to suggest that your bring photocopies of your passport, plane tickets, and hotel reservations. We realize you probably won't do that, but don't come crying to us when the Moncton Place Hotel has no idea who you are.

Note for American travellers: As of 2018, your driver's licence will not be valid in Canada. Upon arriving in Canada, U.S. visitors will be required to take a short written exam on driving rules and practices, leave the country, and return three months later to take their road test. If they pass, they will be allowed to drive north of the border, as long as a licenced Canadian is in the passenger seat.

• Children

There are no laws explicitly prohibiting bringing your children into Canada, although you may have to endure them constantly asking, "Why didn't we go to Hawaii?" Taking kids through Canada is a challenge, as every natural wonder is surrounded by countless wave pools, go-kart tracks, and laser tag arenas, which—let's be honest—are kinda more fun.

• Older People

It's okay to travel with older people—just remember they're gonna wanna stop in *every* boring store and read *every* placard in *every* museum. While you may want to see the Last Spike, older members of your party may wish to take a picture of every single spike along the railroad.

- **Groceries**

Canada is the land of self-service groceries. Customers are now expected to bring their own bags, do their own checkout, and pay with their own money. By the summer of 2017, Canadians will be required to make their own checkout-line grocery-divider thingimabobs.

Also, if you're travelling from a country that has a famous delicacy, could you please bring some? We're dying for some Trader Joe's cookie butter, or those Italian Christmas cakes, or a jar of weird British mint cream.

Finally, in Canada, hygiene products like soap and deodorant are widely available. Hint, hint.

TESTIMONIAL

"I went travelling to find myself. I found Canada instead."

MISSING GUY FROM
NEW ZEALAND

- **Health Needs**

Don't bring any medicine. Ours is free. Pills shoot out of fire hydrants and flood the streets.

Before You Leave

Before entering Canada, it's important to be immunized against the following conditions:

- Butter Rump
- Hat Hair
- Cackle Cough
- The Sniffles
- Mushaboom
- Sore Hips
- West Edmonton Malaria
- Freckles
- Mullets
- Cigarette Dangles
- Advanced Irritable Syndrome
- Bachman Turner Overbite
- The Shoe Flu

Canada's Service Hotlines

Most people only know about calling 911 for an emergency and 411 for information. Did you know about Canada's other service hotlines?

911: Emergency services
There's a fire. My husband is having a heart attack. I'm being murdered.

811: Non-emergency medical
I have a fever. Is this milk okay to drink? I don't feel like playing tennis.

711: 7-Eleven hotline
My Slurpee is melting. Where's the closest 7-Eleven that sells Nibs? Is a Mac's a 7-Eleven?

611: Emergency bear reporting
There's a bear in my yard. There's a bear getting close to a school. A bear stole my car.

511: Non-emergency bear reporting
I see a bear and it's such a beautiful animal, I needed to tell somebody and nobody is around so I called you.

411: Information
What's the phone number for Quiznos? Do you know how late Quiznos is open? Does Quiznos still exist?

311: Municipal issues
The traffic lights are out on my street. My garbage wasn't picked up. What's the mayor really like?

211: Lost sunglasses and keys hotline
Do you know where I left my sunglasses? Can you remember if I had my keys at lunch? Could you check around your office for my car keys?

111: Compliment line
Tell me I'm great. Do you think I look good in this shirt? Help, there's a handsome man trapped in my mirror!

011: Hotline hotline
What's the number for 911? Which one is 611 again? Have you seen my sunglasses? Oh, sorry—wrong number.

Travel Advisories

Canada is generally considered a safe place, but exercising caution, especially where your health or money is concerned, is always smart. In crowded areas, it's a good idea to conceal your valuables either in a money belt, under a neck brace, or in a small balloon that you've swallowed.

In order to ensure that your credit cards work in Canada, notify your bank that you're leaving the country. Calling your bank is also a great way to hear 40 minutes of acoustic guitar hold music. And remember: Your call will be monitored for quality assurance purposes.

- **Crime**

From the moment you arrive in Canada, you are subject to Canadian laws. This means no more potty mouth, roughhousing, horseplay, tomfoolery, clowning around, or shenanigans.

For a realistic look at Canada's justice system, track down a copy of *Bon Cop, Bad Cop,* the highest grossing Canadian movie of all time.

- **In Case of Emergency**

Nobody ever plans a trip with the expectation that the worst will happen, but it's best to be prepared. In case of medical emergency, fire, or violent crime, call 911 immediately. Professional emergency workers will be dispatched right away. Although beware—

Canadians operate at an elevated level of politeness that may work to your disadvantage. While the average passerby is more than willing to help, nobody would want to embarrass you by pointing out that your coat is on fire.

- **Imprisonment**

There are two types of Canadian jail: *jail* jail and the drunk tank. We don't know too much about *jail* jail, but from what we hear, the drunk tank is actually pretty fun. Kyle once ended up in the drunk tank, and he said it wasn't too bad. The cops were mostly pretty nice, and it didn't go on his record or anything.

NOTE: Nobody ever really plans on ending up in the drunk tank, but as a precaution, many Canadians simply bring a pillow along with them when they hit the bars. Visitors are encouraged to do the same.

While Canadian police wear uniforms, as of 2014 police officers in Saskatoon observe "casual Friday." So if you're pulled over by a guy wearing a Hawaiian shirt in an unmarked police car, don't worry—it's a police officer.

The Internet

The Internet is relatively new to Canada. Until just a few years ago, email, Google searches, weather reports, and cat videos were still being delivered by Canada Post. Now a wide variety of three Internet providers proudly offer the world's most expensive—and slowest—connection to the web.

Canada has permission to access almost all of the information the web has to offer, but be warned: geo-blocking is one of the most popular pastimes in the country. If you've chosen to visit Canada because you want to stream the newest music videos or Super Bowl commercials, you are travelling to the wrong place.

Television

To be clear, Canada has televisions. Meaning it has the boxes that play television shows. It has long been a belief that Canada also makes television programs, but these are very hard to come by. Local knowledge dictates that most shows worth watching in Canada are provided by American broadcasters.

WARNING: You may find yourself watching a television show that you assume is real, presented by a U.S. network, when all of a sudden a character will spit out an undeniable "ooot" or "aboot," or, even worse, a supposed Chicago street scene is ruined by a passing Toronto streetcar. When this happens, stay calm—you've stumbled on a Canadian show. Simply change the channel until you're certain you're watching a program made with a budget over $150,000.

If you're watching a period piece with the word "Wind," "Road," "Green," or "Mysteries" in the title, that's also a Canadian program.

Canadian Money

If you're travelling with any currency above a value of $10,000, you must declare it to Canada Customs at the border. The officer will likely be very impressed, and may even ask to take a selfie with the actual cash money. Also, let us know. We'd like to get a taste.

Canada's currency is called the "dollar," which is pronounced "dollar." A one-dollar coin is called a "loonie," a two-dollar coin is a "toonie," and a nine-dollar coin is a "hoonie noonie." New coins are minted daily to reflect the Queen's almost endless supply of new hats.

Travel Tip

Remember, you can't visit all of Canada in one day. It's best to break your trip up into manageable chunks. In fact, the Olde English meaning of "province" is "manageable chunk."

Unit Conversion

It can be difficult to adjust to the metric system if you come from the one country that doesn't use it. Here's a tip: The words "metre" and "litre" can be used interchangeably. Graham the Gram is Canada's official metric mascot. He made his debut at the 1974 Measuring Games.

Canada also uses a number of other unit measures that you'll want to familiarize yourself with before you arrive:

1 Kilometre = 0.621 Miles

1 Litre = 0.264 Gallons

1 Kilo = An amount of drugs the police would show off after a bust

10 Degrees Celsius = 1 Pretty Nice Day

1 Quartz = 2 Quarts

1 Baker's Dozen = 13 Doughnuts

1 Banker's Dozen = 13 Dollars

1 Uvula = That hangy-down thing at the back of your throat

1 *Dragon's Den* = 1 *Shark Tank*

Canadian bills have several security features. The best way to test for authenticity is to run over a bill with a lawnmower. If it gets shredded into a thousand pieces, it's real.

For those who are travelling with large amounts of cash, we always advise that you don't flash it around in public. Consider travellers' cheques, especially if you'll be visiting in 1988.

If you really must have cash, exchanging foreign money is a breeze. Bring a briefcase full of your country's currency to any Canadian post office. The postal workers will exchange your money for a collectible edition of Shania Twain postage stamps. You can use these stamps to write to the bank and ask for some real money.

|||||||||||||||||||||||||||||||||||||||||||||||||||||||||||||||||||||||||||||||||||||||
PLACES TO GO: O CANADA!

- **Parliament Hill**

These stone buildings in Ottawa are some of Canada's most iconic symbols. Walking through these hallowed halls, you're instantly awestruck at the rich history of the world's 109th oldest country. The building features carvings and stained glass windows depicting the nation's history, as well as oak doors, for that oaky smell.

If you're looking for ideas to decorate your foyer, this is the place for you! It has 19 more foyers than the White House, twice as many as the Kremlin, and a third as many as Buckingham Palace. So, how many foyers does it have? (Pssst ... It's 22.)

The building was built in the Modern Gothic Revival style, so make sure you dress in your Gothic clothing: black cloaks, fingerless gloves, and plenty of eyeliner.

Travel Tip

Aluminum cans are currency in Canada. If you find yourself 5 or 10 cents short when making a purchase, you CAN always pay with a CAN.

Tours

For politicos, a guided tour is a must. It's the only way to get full access to the House of Commons. Maybe you'll catch a glimpse of lawmakers debating a piece of legislation, not listening to one another, and congratulating themselves by clapping, pounding on their desks, and yelling, "hear, hear," or jeering opponents by hissing and sarcastically clicking their tongues. It's a beautiful thing to see democracy at work.

And visit the Senate on Wednesdays for 99-cent wings and oil wrestling.

Statues

If you take a walk around the Parliament grounds, you'll see that the buildings are surrounded by a series of wonderful sculptures depicting the Fathers of Confederation and some famous historical figures and moments, including:

- John A. Macdonald
- Laura Secord and the Butter Bite Riots
- Louis Vuitton
- Simon Fraser and the Unfrozen Tree
- The Horse on Horseback
- John Diefenbaker
- The Rusty Dilettante Affair
- Canada Hat

• Golf Course National Park · Prince Edward Island

Dramatic cliffs rise from turquoise waters along the 18 majestic fairways of Canada's most beautiful and exclusive National Park. Ancient trees block your approach, while diverse wetlands and deep bunkers house plenty of local wildlife. Native species include the red-faced boomer, the drunken whooper, and Dean, who has been cutting the greens a little too long lately.

While every other National Park in Canada costs between $0 and $57 for an annual pass, Golf Course National Park visitors pay a one-time $70,000 fee, plus $350 monthly and a reasonable per-use cost. Plan your trip early because there is an eight-year waitlist.

Amenities

The facilities at Golf Course National Park make every other national park look like a pile of puke. Most National Parks have campsites, snack bars, and maybe indoor washrooms. Golf Course has a clubhouse, a dining room, a cigar room, motorized

Entrance to Golf Course National Park

carts, caddies, locker rooms, patios, a pro shop, and a 19th hole. Take that, Bruce Peninsula and your crummy visitors' centre! Sit on it, Forillon and your self-service laundry!

History
Golf Course is the only National Park that is also a National Historic Site, because of that one time Barry hit a hole-in-one.

• Turks and Caicos
Turks and Caicos is a group of islands located in the Caribbean Sea, a short six-hour plane ride from Toronto (nine if you stop in Miami). The islands are populated almost entirely by Canadian vacationers, along with a few local bartenders, tour guides, masseuses, and chambermaids. There may be other residents,

but it's hard to see over the walls of the resorts, especially if you have reservations for the all-you-can-eat lobster buffet. While it's not official, we're hoping the government will have come to their senses and made it the 11th province by the time this book is published.

This Ain't Your Daddy's Canada

Turks and Caicos receives 99 percent of Canada's annual sunlight and produces 100 percent of Canada's annual conch shells. However, it only produces 3 percent of Canada's annual reggae music, with the other 97 percent produced by cover bands at the University of Waterloo.

Don't Pack!

Flying from Toronto in the middle of winter? Follow the lead of every single other person on your flight, and wear shorts and flip-flops to the airport. "Did they leave their coats in the parking lot?" you'll ask. "Did they get dropped off and race through the curbside slush with bare legs?" We may never know, but straw hats and colourful sarongs can be purchased at Pearson International's many kiosks.

Did You Know?

Until last year the Canadian government required all businesses to impose a strict "No Shoes, No Shirt, No Service" policy. Often viewing this as an archaic rule, Canadians collectively rejoiced upon learning the law would no longer be enforced. To experience progress at work, why not go shopping for a Slurpee while barefoot or head to Kinkos for some topless photocopying?

Canada Before

Canada After

LANGUAGE **SOCIAL NORMS**

THE

SEA SHANTIES MONARCHY

CANADIAN

COBBLESTONES FRANCOPHONES

PEOPLE

CITIZENSHIP DAVE

Who Are They?

HUMAN BEING: A man, woman, or child of the species *Homo sapiens,* distinguished from other animals by superior mental development, power of articulate speech, and upright stance. CANADIANS: Human beings.

There's a famous lyric from an old Canadian sea shanty that reads,

Hidda la laddie. Hidda la lee,
hidda la laddie, dooda la lee.
Hoppa la dipply, piddily pop,
hidda la laddie,
hippily scott.

Although this song has absolutely nothing to do with the Canadian people, it should be noted that a Canadian person wrote it. Someone actually sat down and wrote those words. So the point is, it takes all kinds of people to make a country.

Generally, Canadians are a kind, intelligent, hardy bunch of folks who are genuinely interested in where you are visiting from. However, do not expect the conversations to last very long, as small talk is not their strength.

When excited, Canadians are known to release primal hoot and holler sounds like "ah hooooooo" or "yip yip ya ooooo." This hooting and hollering typically occurs on the Friday of a long weekend or when they go camping. Public displays of displeasure, however, are not very common; most Canadians choose to do their grumbling in the privacy of their own homes. The only time Canadians will publicly show they are aggravated is when they are made to wait in lines.

The map below will help you better understand what types of people live in Canada and where.

IIIIIIIIIIIIIIIIIIIIIIIIIIIIIIIIIIIIIIIIIIIIIIIIIIIIIIIIIIIIIIIIIIIIIIIIIIIIIIIIIIIIIIIII
PLACES TO GO: OLD TOWNS, CANADA

- ### Old Town · Canada
No trip to Canada is complete without visiting our "Old Town" region. Yes, Canada is a relatively young nation compared to most other countries, but that doesn't mean we don't have historic older buildings, and most of those are located in Old Town. Get your cameras because some of these buildings are OVER a hundred years old.

What to See
Old buildings! Or at least *older* buildings. Some of our older buildings predate the automobile! Although most don't.

What to Do
Why not hop on a horse-drawn carriage and take a step back in time to see what Canada was like before the television show *Webster*? Some of the buildings in Old Town display the earliest examples of vinyl siding technology in Canada. If you lift up the carpeting in many of these buildings, you will be delighted to find hardwood.

TESTIMONIAL

"Where is everybody?"

TRAVELLER FROM BEIJING

- ### Victoria · British Columbia
Situated on the southern tip of Vancouver Island is the charming city of Victoria. Named after Queen Victoria of Great Britain, the city is often referred to as the London of Canada, not to be confused with London, Ontario, which is also the London of Canada. A wander through any of Victoria's cobblestone lanes, and one can't help but feel that they have been transported to Jolly Old England but without all the bad teeth and confusing currency. If you've ever wanted to visit London but the thought of a nine-hour flight

Victoria, British Columbia

gives you the "collywobbles," then Victoria, BC, may be the perfect place for you.

What to Do

Ride double-decker buses, enjoy bangers and mash, or simply get cheeky with a cobbler. If tea is your passion, don't forget to pack your favourite cup and saucer, because, as per municipal law, every second business in Victoria is a tea room.

NOTE: Your cellphones will be useless here, as all local calls are to be made from red phone boxes. Hellos and goodbyes are "allo allo" and "pip pip," and if it all feels a little overwhelming, just keep calm and carry on.

What You Need to Know

Having a familiarity with the family tree of the British monarchy is definitely recommended. On multiple occasions you will find yourself engrossed in conversations about the Queen and her family. Having a firm grasp on who Camilla Parker Bowles is and why King Edward VIII abdicated the throne for Wallis Simpson will definitely come in handy. Also it is a common courtesy to refer to local men as "gov'nor" and local ladies as "lass" or "hag," depending on their general demeanour.

Where to Stay

A Tudor-style bed and breakfast is definitely the way to go, and in Victoria one will certainly not be hard to find. That way when you're knackered from a day of searching for bits and bobs, you can kip down for the night and wake up to some complimentary bubble and squeak on a crumpet. Or just rent a room in a castle.

• Quebec City · Quebec

Quebec City, nestled between the Saint Lawrence River and the Laurentian Mountains, is one of Canada's most beautiful cities.

Peace of Mind

No matter where you go in Canada, every place is required by law to be equipped with:

- A defibrillator
- Postal delivery
- Pens
- Day beds
- Free lunch
- A women's washroom
- Bushes for the men
- Yarn
- Name tags
- A buddy
- A spotter
- Music
- A cellphone zone

A large part of Quebec City's beauty comes from its heritage. While many cities have maintained their heritage by keeping a few cobblestone streets intact, Quebec City is the only one built entirely out of cobblestones. From the tourist district to the loading docks, every street is cobblestone. And it's not just the streets: fortified walls, buildings, even parking meters are all made out of small, bumpy rocks. Whether you're riding a horse carriage through the park or just pushing a shopping cart through Costco, buckle up—it's gonna be a bumpy ride. Because of the cobblestones.

I'm Confused

No, you're not seeing double. The city is actually called Quebec City, Quebec. In fact, residents of the city take pride in being twice as Québécois as everyone else in the province. Whatever is true of the province of Quebec is twice as true of Quebec City. They speak double French (Franççais), they're twice as romantic, and they smoke four cigarettes at a time instead of two.

|||||||||||||||||||||||||||||||||||||||||||||||||||||||||||||||||||||||||||||||||||

Stages of Life

When interacting with a Canadian, it's important to try to see the world from their perspective. If you want to know where they are coming from, know that they are all going through one of these stages.

- **Infancy (0–1 year)**

It's often said that Canadians learn to skate before they learn to walk. That's ludicrous. Who's going to buy tiny skates that the kid is just going to grow out of? Instead, this stage of life is characterized by helplessness and crying.

> **Travel Tip**
>
> A scarf is a versatile travel tool. Use it for keeping warm, for sun protection, as a towel or eye mask, or to annoy your wife by doing that thing where you pull it back and forth between your legs in a sexy but funny way.

- **Toddlerhood (2–4 years)**

During this stage, Canadians take a huge developmental leap in thought, movement, and language. For the first time, they realize they have power over their surroundings, and they become aware that they are in fact Canadian. It's also around the time when they start throwing Canadian fits and Canadian tantrums.

- **Childhood (5–11 years)**

This stage of a Canadian's life is defined by their entrance into school. They learn everything from pickling to jarring—the different types of jars, parts of a jar, lids for jars, jar labels—and math.

- **Adolescence (12–17 years)**

This is an important developmental stage, as Canadians learn to balance their academic lives, their family lives, their social lives, and, for the first time, their romantic lives. Most kissing happens after the "big game," the "big concert," the "big dance," or the "big science fair."

- **Young Adulthood (18–25 years)**
  After high school, Canadians are free to explore a fruitful postsecondary education, where they will form lifelong friendships, carouse with paramours old and new, perform chemical experiments within themselves, and eat macaroni in basement apartments.

- **Adulthood (26–39 years)**
  This is the time when Canadians go to dinner with their parents and when the cheque comes they proudly say, "Guys, I got this one." They start careers, get married, have children, and talk about how crazy real estate prices have gotten.

- **Middle Age (40–64 years)**
  This is the main time for a person to be a Canadian. It's finally appropriate to be in Canada and to be seen doing Canadian things with Canadian people.

- **Old Age (65–200+ years)**
  Canadians spend this period "semi-retired," meaning they still go into the office a couple times a week but nobody knows why. Regardless of how many times they've been shown, understanding how to update an iPad or send a text message becomes very challenging during this phase.

Canadian Bodies

The Canadian body is no different from the American, Russian, French, or any other body, for that matter. But the words Canadians use to refer to their body parts are unique. A Canadian may complain about an ache in his "bonker" or a twist in her "noodlies," and it's easy to feel stupid if you don't know what they're talking about. Use these diagrams to get up to speed.

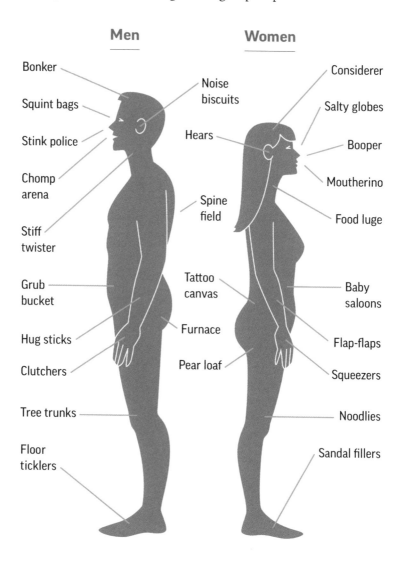

Men

Bonker

Squint bags

Stink police

Chomp arena

Stiff twister

Grub bucket

Hug sticks

Clutchers

Tree trunks

Floor ticklers

Noise biscuits

Hears

Spine field

Tattoo canvas

Furnace

Pear loaf

Women

Considerer

Salty globes

Booper

Moutherino

Food luge

Baby saloons

Flap-flaps

Squeezers

Noodlies

Sandal fillers

Canadians at Work

Even if they can retire, Canadians are refusing to do so in favour of rolling up their sleeves to grind it out until death. These are a people that love to work.

A majority of Canadians consider themselves to be blue- or white-collar workers, while others simply wear clerical, masonic, Nehru, or ruff collars while they work. A small but significant part of the workforce identifies as being hot under the collar. A large percentage of the population makes collars for a living.

The average household income is about $75,000 per year, which coincidentally is the exact amount of money required to buy a collar business.

Canadians at Play

Although not as fun-motivated as their American counterparts, Canadians have been known to let their hair down and throw caution to the wind. In fact, that is something a lot of people do for fun: throw things into the wind. Canada ranks as one of the top 500 countries when it comes to their fun-times-per-citizen ratio. It's easy to tell when a Canadian is having fun. They wear a wide and visible grin, often exclaiming things like "This is *fun!*" or "I'm having a fun time right now!" or simply "Hey, *fun!*"

II

THINGS CANADIANS DO FOR FUN

Strolling

Perhaps the most popular form of fun in the country is strolling. Canadians love to stroll. Although strolling is technically not even legal, these laws are rarely enforced, and it is not uncommon for people to stroll around the block, to the store, through the park, around the lake, or to the corner. Most folks only stroll socially—on weekends or at parties—but some people are chronic strollers and need to stroll immediately after waking up.

Beer Drinking

This is pretty much a no-brainer. When Canadians are drinking a beer, they are most definitely having fun! Of course there are exceptions to the rule—sometimes a beer is consumed in anger, in panic, or as an act of civil defiance—but more often than not, drinking beer as a Canadian is purely an act of fun.

TESTIMONIAL

"Holy crap, they have a lot of rocks."

KYLE FROM PANAMA

Talking about Weather

One of the things that Canadians love to do for fun is talk about the weather. If a Canadian hasn't had a weather-based conversation within the last 24 hours, they may be depressed. If you want to have fun with a Canadian, tell them that the local weather forecast called for sunshine tomorrow. This will start a lengthy but energized conversation about the inaccuracy of meteorology and the general futility of local news.

Hot Tubbing

Canadians are notorious hot tubbers. Leading the world in hot tubs per capita, what Canada lacks in outdoor pools it makes up for in hot, bubbling communal tubs. It's not unusual for a Canadian to spend up to two-thirds of adult life in a deep soak while jets pummel their back. It's common knowledge that in Canada, after important business meetings or when political alliances

have been forged, all parties involved will celebrate with a deep, relaxing soak. Most Canadian boardrooms and courtrooms come fully equipped with a 10-person tub and towel rack.

Bonfires

All along Canada's beaches and throughout its wooded regions, groups of Canadians huddle in semicircle around bonfires. Often these "good fires" are composed of driftwood and dry brush, but when it's time to kick the fun up a notch, all bets are off. When Canadians are truly having fun at a fire, you will see them burning everything from lawn chairs to an old fence. As the fire fun reaches its peak, Dave or Trent will attempt to jump the fire but will roll their ankle, and that's how you know bonfire fun is over.

NOTE: Bonfires aren't allowed during forest-fire season, which now runs from February to December in most regions.

Other popular pastimes include:

- Pickling
- Historical research
- Beachcombing
- Crokinole
- Capture the flag
- Bird herding
- Bean-sack shoe pong
- Napping

|||||||||||||||||||||||||||||||||||||||||||||||||||||||||||||||||||||||||||||||||||||||||||||||||||||

Fashion

The Canadian fashion industry is quite small, but that's not to say that Canadians do not wear clothes. They do. Informed by the climate, most of the country's designers focus on the four pillars of Canadian fashion: Coat Couture, Lake Clothes, Sturdy 'n' Purdy, and To the Max.

Every spring the elite of the Canadian fashion industry gather in Mississauga, Ontario, to discuss the latest trends, share designs, and livestream New York Fashion Week on Jeanne Beker's laptop. From there they take two to three years to come up with designs the Europeans have already forgotten.

Notable Canadian designers include Cathy, Gary, Naseem, Cory, Bruce, Chen, Bill, and Kim.

Napping at your desk is encouraged in Canada

Social Norms Unique to Canada

- Taking off your shoes when arriving at someone's house is very common. No matter how disgusting the floor may be, leaving your shoes on could be interpreted as a declaration of war.
- It's customary for the youngest passenger on an elevator to stand facing the opposite direction from everyone else.
- Limousines do not represent wealth; rather, they are simply vessels in which intoxicated Canadian men and women celebrate their remaining days of unmarried life.

- Always apologize when someone opens the door for you.
- Not only is it unlucky to wear shorts after Thanksgiving, it can be deadly.
- Kissing in public is tolerated but makes most Canadians extremely uncomfortable.
- Swearing must always be done at a whisper or at full volume.
- Eye rolling is quite common, especially when referring to "you know who."
- Talking loudly is strictly forbidden.

Language

Canada has two official languages: English and French. English is the most commonly spoken language in most regions, while French is the main language in Quebec and in some areas of Ontario, New Brunswick, and Manitoba. Although it is not necessary to be fluent in both languages, many Canadians pride themselves on knowing "a little bit" or "un petit peu" of both. Below are some useful phrases in both French and English that will help give the impression you're bilingual.

Hello	Bonjour
Where's the bathroom?	Où se trouvent les toilettes?
Do I need a key for the bathroom?	Ai-je besoin d'une clé pour la salle de bain?
Ok, I don't need a key. If it's locked, someone is in there. Ok.	Ok , je ne pas besoin d'une clé. S'il est verrouillé quelqu'un est là-dedans. D'accord.
What could they possibly be doing in there? It's been 10 minutes.	Que pourraient-ils être en train de faire là-bas? Cela fait 10 minutes.
Do you guys have another bathroom?	Avez-vous les gars ont une salle de bain?
I have an overactive bladder and need in the bathroom now.	J'ai une vessie hyperactive et besoin dans la salle de bain maintenant.
Thank you for letting me use the staff bathroom.	Je vous remercie de me laisser utiliser la salle de bain du personnel.
Neat. Who knew the Starbucks employee bathrooms were so nice.	Soigné. Qui savait que les salles de bains des employés de Starbucks étaient tellement gentils.

Canadians having fun

Canadians not having fun

AIR TRAVEL **CAR RENTALS**

TRANSPORTATION

RAILROADS ROAD TRIPS

AND

HOTELS **HOSTELS**

ACCOMMODATION

SHERPAS CARPETS

Transportation

SAY WHAT YOU will about transportation, it gets you where you're going. And in this crazy, mixed-up world, that's more than you can say about a lot of things. With all of Canada's rugged terrain, it's no surprise that Canadians have invented four major modes of transportation: the canoe, the dogsled, the snowmobile, and those sneakers with wheels in the heels. Additionally, Canadians are responsible for attaching robotic arms to pre-existing vehicles on this planet and beyond.

Making your way across Canada should be easy, whether via air, land, water, ice (which is water), or snow (which is water on land).

Air Travel

Canada's airports are among the busiest in the world. In 2016, nearly 100 million people travelled through Canadian airports, and that's not including people who just came to buy duty-free perfume.

When planning a trip to Canada, make sure you arrive in Brandon Municipal Airport in Brandon, Manitoba. It's a little out of the way, but they make this incredible beef dip. Or, wait.

No. Maybe that's Thunder Bay International Airport. The server there, her name's Marie, and she's this classic diner waitress. You'll know her when you see her because ... Oh no, it's not Marie. It's Sault Ste. Marie Airport. The server's name is Brandon. Anyway, that's some free advice.

Calgary Airport (YYC) has recently knocked off longtime champ Pierre Elliott Trudeau Airport (YUL) to win the Best Airport Carpet award at Canada's annual Ruggies, the flooring awards hosted by Alan Thicke. Critics called Calgary's brown swirls "avant-garde," "surreal," "brown," and "easy to walk on."

As with almost everything else these days, plane tickets are sold online. The Internet is so amazing! There's a whole "web site" devoted to crackers too! But that's beside the point. Plane tickets are available from a number of sites: Wingzly, Travllr, Triptrap, Aeosz, and Planehumpers, just to name a few.

TESTIMONIAL

"I was disappointed that they didn't give us a lei upon arrival."

GUY WHO NORMALLY GOES TO HAWAII

Air Travel Slang

If you want to score some extra points with your fellow travellers, memorize these terms so you can talk like a real Canadian flyer.

- **Airplane**: This is what you sit on when you fly. It's the wingy thingy.
- **Cheese Plate**: A $14 box of ice-cold Cheddar cubes.
- **Landers and Leavers**: Arrivals and Departures.
- **Ma'am**: What airline staff call you to let you know you're being rude.
- **Reclining**: The seat feature that makes your life 1 percent better, and someone else's life 100 percent worse.
- **Rollie Boys**: Suitcases with wheels.
- **Sir**: see Ma'am.
- **Tomato Juice**: The only drink available on the plane.

There are still old-fashioned ways to get flying, such as using a travel agent, finding plane tickets on the street, or bringing bus tickets to the airport and just playing dumb until you get on a plane.

Renting a Car

Although children can vote at 18 and consume alcohol by 19, full adulthood is not recognized in Canada until a person is 25. This is the age when someone is deemed mature enough to rent a car.

Locations are fairly convenient and are predictably expensive. Note that if you book a car from a website you feel offers a reasonable rate, you will get hammered with fees when picking up the keys. And even if you are 100 percent sure you are covered, when you decline the insurance, the clerk will give you this look that's like "Jeeeeez...risky!" Remember, everyone will know you tried to save money by renting a sub-compact, so cough up the extra 10 bucks a day and rent a 'Stang.

TESTIMONIAL

"A cab ride from Windsor to the Okanagan cost way more than we expected."

NICE COUPLE FROM CHICAGO

Road Games

Spice Up Your Drive with This Game of "I Spy Trans-Canada Highway Bingo":

B	I	N	G	O
Roadkill	An abandoned Blockbuster Video	An oversized Adirondack chair	One of those station wagons where the kids are facing backward	Hitchhiker with hook hand
Your friend Derek	Bigfoot	One shoe	Roadside canola-oil stand	Discarded wig
A 1975 Bricklin	Wind turbines	FREE SPACE	A big weirdo	Cows whispering to each other
An RV pulling another RV	Two deer sitting on chairs like people	10 cemeteries in 10 minutes	A city named after another, better city	Beautiful old farm used for hipster weddings
Exit ramp	Dog wearing glasses	Entrance ramp	Sweet ramp for doing jumps off	IKEA

It's long been believed that, like in England, Canadians drive on the left side of the road. This is not the case. But as many roads in Canada are single lane, it is quite common for motorists to drive in the *centre* of the road. On most Canadian highways the average speed limit is between 80 and 110 kilometres per hour, which may seem fast, but for European visitors that's about half the speed you're used to. In the summer months, speed limits don't really matter, as everywhere you drive you'll inevitably be stuck behind a camper going 50.

Rail Journeys

Canada has a large railway system dedicated primarily to cargo trains. Although it is believed that the country has passenger trains as well, little is known about them. You can for sure take a train from Montreal to Toronto—that much we know—but can you take a train from Saskatoon to Calgary? Maybe? If you want to traverse the country by train, you're more than welcome to give it a shot, but be prepared to hop a boxcar or two if you want to get to Nelson.

Public Transit

Good news! Most Canadian cities have public transit. Bad news! Buses make up a majority of it, and no matter where you are, a city bus is still a city bus. As with most city buses, making eye contact with strangers is strictly forbidden, and if there is room on the bus, NEVER sit too close to another passenger. Personal body space is coveted in Canada; invading it may cause the victim to apologize.

Major cities that offer subway, metro, or light rapid transit service include Vancouver (Sky High Train), Calgary (Iron Horse), Edmonton (The Great One), Toronto (Red Rocket), Ottawa (The Nap Trax), and Montreal (The Sex Train).

IIIIIIIIIIIIIIIIIIIIIIIIIIIIIIIIIIIIIIIIIIIIIIIIIIIIIIIIIIIIIIIIIIIIIIIIIIIIIIIIIIIIIIIIIIIIIIIIIII
PLACES TO GO: PEAKS AND VALLEYS

- **Alberta Badlands**

Sitting at #4 on our Gotta See list: the Alberta Badlands. Every year, thousands of tourists flock to Alberta's badlands to visit Drumheller's Royal Tyrell Museum of Paleontology. The museum's dinosaur exhibits are sure to dazzle your eyes, challenge your mind, and tire out your nine-year-old son, Brayden.

Founded in 1985, the museum contains 130,000 fossils, reconstructed skeletons, lifelike dioramas, and a not-to-be-missed cafeteria which boasts some of Drumheller's finest chili. The museum received its "Royal" designation in 1993, after Queen Elizabeth saw *Jurassic Park,* which she declared to be "totally kickass." That same year, the house from *Mrs. Doubtfire* also received a "Royal" designation.

Hours are 10 a.m. to noon, and 2 p.m. to 5 p.m., all day in the summer, shorter hours on Sunday, never on Monday afternoons. Upon arrival, don't forget to exchange your money for Dino-bucks (1 Canadian dollar = 1 Dino-buck).

Fun Fact

Before becoming the Raptors, Toronto's NBA franchise was named the Toronto Royal Tyrell Museums.

What to Look Out For

Due to the interactive nature of the exhibits, it's easy to get a little too familiar with the dinosaurs. While most visitors intend to vandalize the museum, that's actually forbidden. Keep an eye out for a crew of undercover security guards dressed as small dinosaurs (deinonychus, tarbosaurus, etc.), on hand to prevent you from surfing down an apatosaurus's neck or carving your initials into a trilobite.

What to Bring

This one is a no-brainer: bring one of your shale guidebooks from home. You'll look quite foolish if you're the only member of your tour group without a shale guidebook for classifying fossilized deposits of shale based on its varying levels of shininess.

Hoodoo You Think You Are?

When you're done checking out the sites, head over to Hoodoo's Bar and Grill for their nightly drink specials, hot wings, and house band, Dave Hoodoo and the Voodoo Hoodoo Dino Doodoo.

- **Porcupine Hill**
The wild and rugged landscape of the Canadian Rockies spans the provinces of British Columbia and Alberta. With

Travel Tip

Waterproof your baseball cap with fibreglass hot-tub resin. That way you can take it off and eat cereal out of it.

over 100 mountain peaks, including the impressive Mount Robson, standing at 3,954 metres, it's a region with mind-blowing wilderness, jaw-dropping wildlife, and endless opportunity for recreational activities—which is why we don't recommend going there. The Rockies are just too darn busy and have become one of the most clichéd destinations in the country. For those travellers looking for a truly unique Canadian experience that satisfies their thirst to see large mounds, we suggest making your way east of the Rockies to the Manitoba–Saskatchewan border, home of Porcupine Hill.

What You Need to Know

With a compelling elevation of about 700 metres, Porcupine Hill ranks as the 5th highest mountain in Manitoba and the

8,628th highest mountain in Canada. If you stacked two Leaning Towers of Pisa on top a horizontal Eiffel Tower, you would still not reach the height of what locals call Pee Pee Hill. After a hike of about 45 minutes, binocular-free views from the summit are reasonably satisfying. You'll be glad you made the five-hour trip to get there.

How to Get There

Board a quick two-hour flight from Toronto to Winnipeg. Car rentals are available at the Winnipeg airport for a fee of about $85 per day (total with insurance coverage: $7,000 per day). Head northwest on Highway 16 for exactly five hours and 12 minutes. As you approach what appears to be a large hill or small mountain, you've arrived at Porcupine Hill.

What to Do There

Climb to the top of Porcupine Hill.

- **Athabasca Glacier**

In the rugged Canadian Rockies at the southern edge of Jasper National Park sits the receding Athabasca Glacier. This 7-kilometre-long expanse of receding ice is one of six principal receding glaciers that together form the receding Columbia Icefield.

Why You Should Go

The Athabasca Glacier is the most visited glacier in North America; however, we can't guarantee it will be around for long, so act quickly. Consider your trip like being at a going-out-of-business sale. This may be one of the last times to actually see ice on the face of Planet Earth.

TESTIMONIAL

"They say mountains are the cathedrals of the wilderness. I agree—like churches, once you've seen one old mountain, you've kinda seen them all."

UNIMPRESSED GUY
FROM NORWAY

What to Do

Take pictures. *Lots* of pictures. Photographs of this melting sheet of ice may be cherished relics for future generations, a way for your grandchildren to see that at one time southern Jasper wasn't just alpine fields of moist pebbles but actually held frozen water, similar to what they might find in their freezers. If freezers are still being used in the future. Photography, however, is only some of the fun that can be had during a visit. Why not simply pull up a folding chair and watch the ice melt, or for those who enjoy a good fitness challenge, bring your running shoes and try to race the receding glacier? It's a good test for even the most seasoned of sprinters.

Travel Tip

You can make your own travel mug out of thermally vacuum-insulated machined stainless steel and a BPA-free moulded spill-proof plastic and silicone lid.

• The Not-So-Great Lakes

For many visitors to Canada, the Great Lakes are an absolute must-see. Situated along Ontario's southern border, the Great Lakes contain one-fifth of the surface fresh water of Planet Earth. However, these tourist magnets can often be a crowded mess of looky-loos in Bermuda shorts trying to canoe their way from Sudbury to Toronto. For visitors wishing to enjoy a lake that's maybe not great but is still pretty good, we recommend the Not-So-Great Lakes.

Where to Find Them

Dotted along the the northern edges of the Great Lakes are thousands of small lakes that are honestly pretty good. We highly recommend lesser-known lakes like Lower Ross Lake, or Bilton Lake and the impressive Gowan Lake.

||||||||||||||||||||||||||||||||||||||||||||||||||||||||||||||||||||||||||||||||||||||||

Accommodation

ACCOMMODATION in Canada is as vast and varied as the landscape it sits upon. The most popular head-resting joints include (in a very particular order) chain motels, motor hotels, fleabag motels, mostly motels, luxury hotels, so-so hotels, used-to-be-good hotels, party hotels, airport hotels, hostel hotels, hostel hostels, hostile hostels, B&Bs, Airbnbs, Land B&Bs, Sea B&Bs, A B&Bs, and A B&Cs.

Most regional tour offices will publish a magazine with a comprehensive list of accommodations in the area. You will find these magazines on the nightstand of the room you have already checked into.

Hotels

The priciest option for accommodation is a hotel. And why not? It's a building full of people who throw towels on the floor, leave food in the hallway, and clog toilets all day long, and somehow everything miraculously ends up clean. Consider whether hotel living is the greatest way to live.

While it feels pretty swanky to spend a night in a hotel, it doesn't have to cost an arm and a leg. When you book your room, ask to be placed on the same floor as the team in town for a pee-wee hockey tournament (there's always one). There's usually a discount for that. Special deals are also often available if you agree to wear the hotel robes in town. And finally, don't forget to tell the concierge it's your honeymoon. That's usually good for free towels.

Did You Know

Canadian hotel breakfasts feature a strip omelette bar—for every topping on your omelette, you must remove an article of clothing.

• **Best Carpet**
Toronto's Royal York Hotel has consistently won the Best Hotel Carpet Ruggie Award. Critics call it "criss-crossed," "flowery," "swirly," and "cushy, but with different types of cushiness."

Youth Hostels

A more affordable option than a hotel room is one of the country's many youth hostels. These dormitory-style accommodations feature bedrooms with between 4 and 24 beds, shared bathrooms, and the maximum legally allowed number of Australians.

Where hotels offer quiet, privacy, and cable TV, hostels have constant noise, accidental nudity, and cable TV. The TV room is communal and someone always wants to watch *TMZ*, because hey, they're on vacation.

Not only are hostels an affordable option because of their lower rates ($35 to $85 a night), many offer you the option to pay with good vibes.

Middle-Aged Hostels

If you want the spirit and fun of a hostel but notice your youth is dwindling every time you look in a mirror, book a bed in one of the country's network of middle-aged hostels. Here, backpackers

between the ages of 40 and 60 share quiet rooms, have earlier bedtimes, and chat about prostate exams and station wagons.

For a few extra dollars, you can get your own lumbar pillow. A few more, and you can have a private bedroom and bathroom. A few more, and you can stay at a hotel.

Airbnb

Apps and the web have made travel a whole lot creepier. The new generation will never know a world where travellers didn't use some stranger's towels. That's what Airbnb is all about. Whether you're a group of rowdy teens looking for a house to trash or a bachelor party looking for a house to trash, Airbnb has something for everybody.

Booking with Airbnb is easy. Email webmaster@airbnb.com with a list of possible travel dates, the kind of vibe you're looking for in a house (funky, random, totally '70s), and some pictures of the kind of chairs you're used to sitting in. They'll email back with a list of houses that match. You then take your money and leave it under a rock that you've both decided on, and voila! You're Airbnb-ing.

II

TOURS

Canada is the perfect place to mosey aimlessly, but tours can take over where your wanderlust ends. Here are a few guided, scenic, and historical tours.

- ### Winnipeg Sherpa · Guided
  When a Mount Everest sherpa married a Canadian woman, he moved to Winnipeg. His guide experience comes through as he gives tours from the Red River to the Nutty Club factory, all while he helps you find shelter from the blistering winds of Portage and Main. Just be aware that while Winnipeg is a flat city, a lifetime on Everest means your guide is constantly seeking opportunities to climb. Whether it's the toboggan hill in Civic Park or the stairs at the MTS Centre, this is a climbing tour—your calves will get jacked.

- ### Trois-Rivières Gum-Tasting Tour · Guided
  Have you ever wondered what the difference is between wintergreen and spearmint? This and many more mysteries of gum will be revealed as you chew your way through Trois-Rivières' picturesque Gum District (*La place de la mâche*). Learn the proper way to unwrap a stick of gum, bubble theory, and whether to pair a fruity or a minty gum with your meal.

- ### Highway 2 between Calgary and Edmonton · Scenic
  The best part of this breathtaking three-hour trip is that drivers only have to turn the steering wheel slightly, once. Although the scenery doesn't change too drastically for 300 kilometres, the stillness of the landscape has a hypnotic effect. Often drivers will feel the sensation of snapping to attention after driving for, like,

A spectacular drive

10 minutes without even realizing it. It's the kind of drive that can lull the wildest of souls. Download the audio tour to hear the names of the various auction yards you'll pass.

- **Newfoundland** · Scenic
Who are we kidding—this place is *gorgeous*. Have you seen those commercials advertising Newfoundland Tourism? Come on! The one with the little redhead kid bouncing around in front of colourful houses? Trust us: just get in a car and drive around this place and pretend you are a Viking discovering a new-found land. That's it. If you don't like what you see, you are insane and should get examined by a medical professional.

- **Leaf Changing in Ontario and Quebec** · Scenic
If you can land in that sweet pocket between when it's crazy hot and when it's crazy cold, you're in the prime window for leaf-changing time. Head over to a forest or a provincial park, stroll around, and watch the leaves change. (NOTE: The leaves only change colour; they don't change into something else, like a bench or a tiger.)

- **Dawson City Tanning Tour** · Historical
Dawson City, Yukon, was the epicentre of Canada's Gold Rush. But what became of the newly minted millionaires who struck it rich panning for gold? They relaxed and got tans in the Land of the Midnight Sun. See all the hot tanning spots off the dusty boardwalk of this ghost town. Find out the horrific answer to the question "What did they use for lotion?"

TESTIMONIAL
"The sky here reaches forever. It actually reached into my pocket and stole five bucks! That's a little joke."
DENNIS, SHANGHAI, CHINA

- **Farms of Saskatchewan** · Guided
Have you ever wanted unlock the magic of Saskatchewan through the eyes of a local? If the answer is yes, then Herb Fleming's guided tour is for you. As the province's self-proclaimed #1 fan of farming, Herb and his 21-day tour put you in the front seat of the farming life. Literally. Over the course of three weeks, you'll have the pleasure of sitting in the cab of Herb's truck as drives around the province showing you some of his favourite farms. Not only will you learn about barns, balers, seeders, silos, combines, tractors, sprayers, quarter-ton trucks, half-ton trucks, and full-ton trucks, but you'll learn how the Roughriders won the 1966 Grey Cup.

||||||||||||||||||||||||||||||||||||||||||||||||||||||||||||||||||||||||||||||||||||||||||||||||

Camping

Canada is bursting with nature, and Canadians love to go camping. From May to September, nature lovers flock to the country's 11 campsites for a chance to sleep on the ground.

For tourists, camping can be a cheap way to experience all that Canadian nature has to offer:

- Beauty
- Guaranteed bears
- Limited cell signal
- Canada's four new constellations: the Haircut, Gwendolyn, Big Dipper 2, and the Six-Star
- Campfire bans
- A shopping cart in the forest

Travel Tip

You'll discover a lot more if you get lost on purpose. You'll probably get lost by accident too, but if anyone asks, you got lost on purpose.

Farmers

Between Canadian cities, there are huge expanses of farmland. If you find yourself travelling from city to city as the sun sets, it's customary to knock on a farmer's door and ask to spend the night. The farmer will lay down some rules, usually involving his daughter, and if you don't obey, chances are you'll wind up with an unbelievable story!

Morning rush hour in Canada

Afternoon rush hour in Canada

4

FESTIVALS SCENIC TOURS

THINGS TO

ARCHITECTURE MUSIC

SEE

FOOD & DRINK MUSEUMS

AND DO

SHOPPING TAXIDERMY

Is It Boring?

HISTORICALLY, PEOPLE came to Canada because they thought there would be things to see and do. And they weren't wrong. From lookouts to cookouts, Canada's seeing and doing infrastructure is well developed. Often travellers to the country will return home complaining that they have actually seen too much.

Some things are better to see, and some things are more worth doing, but overall this section should provide you with all you need to have a satisfactory trip.

WARNING: Nothing listed here can be unseen.

Festivals

It's really hard to avoid festivals in Canada, and that's because during the summer months there are 48 million of them. If you can think of a festival, Canada has it. And if for some reason Canada doesn't have the festival you're looking for, it will bend over backward to create one for you. Festivals are so common that, in some cases, unbeknownst to each other, neighbouring towns will hold the exact same festival at the exact same time.

For example, on July 18th there are 124 Butter Tart Festivals happening in Ontario alone.

- **Folk Fest · Canada-wide**

If there's one type of festival that Canada has dialled, it is the folk festival. Dotted across the country, these events attract thousands of attendees looking to let their hair down and do that weird "sway" type of dancing. A Canadian Folk Fest will no doubt inspire you to say, "Screw it. For the next three days, I'm just gonna sit in this lawn chair, gorge myself on ethically sourced, sustainable churros, and folk out to a banjo collective from Winnipeg." WARNING: At most FFs, you must arrive three days early to obtain a wristband that gets you in line to pick up your laminate badge, which allows you to reserve your spot of grass with a blanket.

TESTIMONIAL

"Canada is like a folk festival, but all the time."

FREE-SPIRITED WOMAN who is always dancing at outdoor concerts while everyone else sits

- **The Swift Current Currant Current Events Festival**

Two things bring Saskatchewaners together: fruit farming and talking about the news. For three weeks every June, Swift Current is the current currant capital of the world. It's a celebration of blackcurrants, red currants, and golden currants, as well as newsworthy current events. Here you can enjoy some blackcurrant jam while a band plays some of the current hits. Or try a red currant pie shaped like your favourite current newsmaker. You won't need to keep track of the current price of the Canadian dollar, though. Here, the only currency is currant seeds.

- **The Calgary Festival of Toronto**

Billed as the Greatest Outdoor Show on Earth, Calgary's Festival of Toronto is world-famous. This 10-day event celebrates all the

things that make Toronto unique to Calgary. The entire city takes on a party atmosphere: offices and restaurants are painted in Bay Street themes, residents dress as Torontonians, and across the city hundreds of "Toronto breakfasts" are held.

- ## The Canmore Scat Festival

Skimminy-bimminy-beep-bop-skaloo! It's time for some scat. While some Canadian metropoli have citywide jazz fests, Canmore, Alberta, blocks off one city block for its annual festival of mouth jazz, better known as "scatting." Every year, the town is inundated with some of the world's best at making noises with their mouths. Book your trip early—scat fans from all over land

in this small town, and the motel fills up pretty quick. Past performers include Scatman Phelps, Scatman Jenkins, and Deion "Scatman" Phelps.

- **Victoria Writers Festival Organizers Festival**
Statistics show that one-third of Canadians are the organizer of a writers' festival. During this three-day event in Victoria, British Columbia, organizers of writers' festivals from all over the country come together to celebrate organizing writers' festivals. Panels include "How to Host a Reading," "Folding Chairs and You," "Where to Have the Book Signing," and "The Best Boxed Wines for Tiny Plastic Cups." Admission includes a tote bag organizer for your writers' festival tote bag collection.

- **The Cranbrook Crantini and Cranberry Festival**

  If cranberry crantinis are your thing, then look no further than the Cranbrook Crantini and Cranberry Festival. In late August, hundreds of crantini enthusiasts converge on this idyllic British Columbia town to swap recipes, slurp crantinis, and celebrate North America's most mysterious berries. Get there early because they often run out of cranberries and have to use figs.

- **Festival de les Cubes de la Glace de Laval**

  In winter, Canadians are always looking for some reason to get out of their fart-filled houses during the four hours of daylight. One of Canada's many winter festivals is this one in Laval, Quebec, which translates to "The Ice Cube Festival." On the frozen 40-acre grounds, festival-goers celebrate the many uses of "nature's pebble," the ice cube. There's chilled lemonade to drink, coffee pots to clean, and cooling packs for achy joints. The festival culminates in the ice cube masquerade, in which participants wear lavish masks made of ice cubes and peacock feathers.

- **Hamilton Buskers Festival**

  The granddaddy of all busking festivals, the Hamilton Buskers Fest features all the usual unusual suspects—guys on stilts, guys painted gold who don't move, guys who play drums on buckets, and guys who juggle while yelling at you. Make sure to bring a pocket full of change to this one: regardless of whether you dislike a particular act, you will be masterfully guilted into putting money in the performer's hat. Take a break from the action by heading to Hammers Tavern for a local concoction called a "Ti-Cat Clamato." It's also a great place to ponder how you can become a busker yourself.

Travel Tip

Avoid the heartache of dropping your phone in the toilet by presoaking all of your electronics before you leave.

- **Kingston Soup Chuck**

  For one day in August, the town of Kingston, Ontario, welcomes visitors to throw cans of tomato soup at one another in an over-sized food fight. Painful? Yeah, but it's fun, right? There are differing theories as to how this festival began, but many believe it pays tribute to a famous incident in Kingston's history when locals tossed cans of soup in Lake Ontario to protest a new soup tax. Unlike Spain's La Tomatina, no food is wasted, as everyone tries to return their dented cans to Loblaws for store credit.

- **Lytton Hot Comedy Festival**

  During the last week of July, the town of Lytton, British Columbia, is Canada's hot spot, with temperatures in the high 30s. That's also the week that the town hosts its comedy fest. Headliners from Canada and around the globe roll into town to perform at the historic Lytton Heater (it used to be "Theater" but the T fell off in a sandstorm). If you like impressions, you'll love hearing a parched comedian's John Wayne impersonation while you wait to hear when the air conditioner will be fixed. You'll be too hot to laugh at the ventriloquist, as you wonder how even a wooden dummy is sweating.

IIIIIIIIIIIIIIIIIIIIIIIIIIIIIIIIIIIIIIIIIIIIIIIIIIIIIIIIIIIIIIIIIIIIIIIIIIIIIIIIIIIIIIIIIIII
PLACES TO GO: THE C'S

• Cabot Trail

John Cabot, for whom the Trail is named, famously quipped upon discovering the area in 1497, "This place is great—I can totally see people from all over the world coming here to enjoy local culture, music, and countless outdoor activities and to attend our local kitchen parties."

The Cabot Trail, a scenic roadway that takes you around the greater part of Nova Scotia's Cape Breton, is one of the most famous drives in Canada (second only to Wayne Gretzky Drive in Edmonton). Visitors to Cape Breton should set aside one to four days to see all the sights along the Cabot Trail. Again, how long you plan for this trip really depends on how many campers going 30 kilometres an hour you plan on getting stuck behind. If you end up at the back of the pack, set aside nine days.

Celtic It!

There are countless cultural experiences along the way but none more popular than Celtic this and Celtic that. Take in a Celtic art gallery, dance a jig to Celtic music at the Celtic festival which happens every Celtic October, visit a Celtic village with Celtic houses, eat Celtic fish, watch a re-enactment of a Celtic wedding, go to a Celtic basketball game, learn Celtic, and buy a Celtic postcard. If you Celtic dream it, the Cabot Trail Celtic has it.

• Churchill Polar Bear Hall of Fame

The town of Churchill, Manitoba, is known as The Polar Bear Capital of the World, with thousands of the bears migrating through town every year on their way to hunt for seals in Hudson Bay. For decades, ecotourists have ridden tundra buggies to catch a glimpse of these arctic beasts, but the recently opened Roar & More Hall of Fame lets "bearheads" see these magnificent creatures in a heated building.

Roar!

You can get up close and personal with some of the greatest polar bears of all time, including Gary the Bear, "Polar" Jonathan Bear, and Arctic Bruce. All the greats have been stuffed and taxidermied to evoke the image of their glory days. You'll see what got Hank "White Paws" Polar Bear his signature nickname, and if it's really true what they said about "Scruffy" Sam Bear—that he was really scruffy.

More!

The Hall of Fame doesn't just show off the bears themselves (although it does have thousands of them); it also has a bunch of "bearaphernalia." Included in the collection is the trophy that Max "Bear Teeth" Bear won for eating all those seals. There are also a few sweaters and vests that bears have accidentally wound up wearing while going through people's garbage.

Travel Tip

When tucking in for the night, always tie your shoes together. If someone steals your shoes while you sleep, they won't just take one—they'll take both.

• The CN Tower

One of Canada's more soft-spoken landmarks, and one of the seven wonders of the world that Stevie Wonder has visited, the CN Tower has come to define the opening credits of most national newscasts. At 1,815 feet in height, this impressive tower is hard to miss while in Toronto. Actually, it's impossible—if you are missing it, you're likely not in Toronto; you're in Oshawa. Check your map.

One of the world's great mysteries

The CN Tower is home to a number of adventure activities. If you're feeling dangerous, a walk across the glass floor is a thrill. If you feel like staying in your shell to avoid personal growth by pushing your own limits, a walk across the regular floor is pretty neat too.

Getting Up There

There are two ways to get up the CN Tower. The first is by purchasing a general admission ticket for approximately $35, hopping on an elevator, and voila, you're at the tippy top of Tower Town.

The second is by locating a great guy named Stu who tends bar at Finny Snackersons, the Irish pub across the street. Stu used to work at the Tower and still has a working fob that gives him access to all the entrances and elevators. For a fee of about 10 bucks and a couple smokes, Stu will let you in. He will also

introduce you to his buddy Gary, who is responsible for making the revolving restaurant spin. For a small fee, Gary will show you how it works.

Tower FAQS

Q: Why did they build the CN Tower?

A: Probably a Mayan thing—Machu Picchu sorta deal. To appease the god of somethin' or other.

Q: Why is it called the CN Tower?

A: The "CN" in "CN Tower" stands for Canadian National, the railway company that built it. Originally, they hoped to be the first railway in the world to successfully park a train vertically. That didn't happen. In many ways, the Tower stands as a representation of their own engineering failures (both the train kind and the other kind).

Q: If the CN Tower could be any other tower, who would it be? And why?

A: Eiffel. For sure. To be able to keep those French hours? Come on, no-brainer!

|||||||||||||||||||||||||||||||||||||||||||||||||||||||||||||||||||||||||||||||||||||||

Best Shopping

Whether you're buying knick-knacks, picking out paddywhacks, or just want to give your dog a bone, Canada is a shopper's paradise. And this old man (the economy) comes rolling home.

Good news for visitors from just about anywhere else in the world: Your money's worth way more than the Canadian dollar, meaning you can comfortably buy about five of everything. But be warned that haggling is not common in Canada. Rather, it's customary to let out an exasperated sigh when told the price of something. If, following that sigh, a clerk refuses to come down in price, the customer should simply apologize, fork over the cash, and quietly huff 'n' puff to themself.

• Shopping Areas

The main shopping area in Canada is the Trans-Canada Highway. Along this 7,800-kilometre promenade, you can find merchants selling everything you'd expect to see in Canada: fine silks, spices, luggage, greeting cards, cork, jewellery shaped like skulls, and prototypes of automobiles.

Another great shopping spot to visit is the third floor of The Bay, where they keep the mattresses. This is also where you'll find the cleanest bathrooms in the country.

• Opening Hours

Canada opens at 8 a.m., when the country's many stores unlock their doors in unison, creating a harmonious "click" that echoes throughout the land. Keen shoppers often line up before the

> ## Insider Tip
>
> If you're travelling with someone who has expensive tastes, the stretch from Winnipeg to Kenora features all the high-end boutiques: Chanel, Fendi, Carl Labouche, Rickety Tickety, Bung Boys, Touchie Touchie, and Moores.

stores open; extremely keen shoppers line up right after the stores close. Between the hours of 2 and 3 p.m., most stores close their door to allow workers to watch their "stories" on television.

- **Refunds**

Most Canadian stores will offer refunds within 30 days with no questions asked, 60 days with 2 questions asked, and 90 days with 4 questions asked.

Must-Visit Stores

- **Pickers Paradise · Ontario**

If you have a strong desire to buy something that was made before today, the best antiques market in the country is in Ontario. This 400,000-square-foot barn is a mothball-scent enthusiast's dream come true and will instantly whisk you down a memory lane of junk. From old coffee tins to old tobacco tins, and from old lozenge tins to old tin toys, Pickers Paradise is the perfect place to buy something that months later will have you asking,

Taxes

Visitors can find Canadian taxes pretty confusing, especially when the price on the label doesn't match the price you pay. Here's a quick look at the fees and taxes you'll pay on goods and services in Canada.

- Tax Tax
- The Other Tax
- Extra Tax
- Surcharge Tax
- Dairy Farmers' Surcharge
- Fuel Surcharge

- Administrative Fees
- Facts Tax
- Network Fee
- Convenience Charge
- Hotel Tax
- Tobacco Tax

"Why did I buy this?" Stay clear of the porcelain doll section, as the lady running it will creep you out with how many times she says, "Isn't she precious?"

Also watch out for counterfeits.

WARNING: This is not a Hudson's Bay blanket.

WARNING: This is not an antique canoe paddle.

WARNING: Gordon Lightfoot never owned this guitar.

• Nancy's Sweatshirts · Alberta

After growing frustrated with being uncontrollably chilled, Canadian Nancy Sheply invented the shapeless cozy sweatshirt in 1985. Today Nancy's Sweatshirts, in Lethbridge, Alberta, stands as a shrine to her practical and life-changing invention. Line up early to buy one of Nancy's bestsellers, a cozy sweatshirt with a cartoon bear holding a flower pot, with a caption that says, "Bear-y Potter."

• Kirk's Work Wearhouse · Lesser Malls

Traditionally, this store supplied clothing to workers in Canada's rough-and-tumble manufacturing and resource industries. As the country's work landscape has moved into the 21st century, this workwear mecca had moved with it. Sure, they still carry steel-toed boots and canvas coveralls, but their offerings have grown to reflect new work realities: slippers for people who work at home, ironic T-shirts for app developers, cardigans for coffee-shop screenwriters, and aprons for artisanal so-and-so's.

• Dan-Yay Leather · Canada-wide

This store is wall-to-wall leather, which is a new type of fabric made out of cow parts. Leather technology is so cutting-edge, most of the products don't even have names yet. Intrigued? This store has everything: leather cases for your feet, leather cases for your hands, leather envelopes for your money, leather blankets with holes for your arms and head, even leather straps to hold up your denim leg tubes.

• Stickz · Ottawa, Ontario

You can't return home to your kids without bringing them some Canadian sticks. Kids love 'em. And while it may be tempting to pick up any of the billion sticks lying around the country, that would be a mistake. At Stickz, a professional sticksmith will fit your child with a custom stick, twig, or branch, based on their measurements, interests, and haircut. They'll even write you a note so you can take your stick through Customs.

• Everythings · Canada-wide

Need to pick up some groceries, sporting goods, and break-fast but don't have time to make three stops? What if you don't have time to even make *one* stop? The country's biggest big-box chain is also the country's only drive-through store. With four-lane aisles, you can peel out by the bananas, three-point turn to the basketball hoops, and do doughnuts past the crullers. The self-checkout aisle is still a clusterfuck.

Standout Strip Malls of the Maritimes

In Canada, the strip mall is the epi-centre of every community. Mall quality may vary from province to province, but without question the country's most spectacular strip malls are in the Maritimes. To get some local flavour, head to these revered landmarks to buy Skittles or souvlaki, practise your stall parking, or just be seen among a crowd of vaping teens. Here are the five shining stars among Maritime strip malls:

Pictou Plaza · New Glasgow, NS
Say hello to the cheery lottery players, and stop at the self-serve nacho stand—the cheese pump is to die for. Grab a Slushie and head to the river to throw sticks at a half-submerged shopping cart.

Red Soil Plaza · Charlottetown, PEI
After taking $40 out of an unaf-filiated ATM, stroll over to the world's smallest pharmacy. This boutique-style apothecary is so exclusive, it has only one box of Band-Aids.

Colchester Commons · Stewiacke, NS

After buying life insurance (the sunbleached posters tell you the broker has been in the community for years), pick up some smokes at the only store in town to offer American Marlboros. Do not fear: visitors no longer have to worry about crowds—not since they put up a handmade sign allowing no more than four high school students at a time.

Place de Plaza · Bouctouche, NB

For some French flavour, the dry cleaner will remove the scent of Gauloises and brie from your beret while you get some sun at Bronzage chez Bruno, the province's most popular tanning salon.

Oromocto Mall · Oromocto, NB

If your identity was stolen at an unaffiliated ATM and your credit cards were frozen, the friendly folks at the cheque-cashing outlet are there to loan you some money at a reasonable rate. Feeling overcaffeinated? Use your windfall to splurge on some water-weakened brew served in an antique 1980s coffee pot, from Mona's, the region's leading doughnut/samosa/egg salad sandwich shop.

- ### Everything Pretzel'd · Cape Breton, Nova Scotia
  The philosophy of this Cape Breton store is that everything is better when it's shaped like a pretzel, and they might be on to something! They have everything from steering wheels to martini glasses, all twisted into pretzels. While you're there, give a toot on the pretzel'd trumpet. The spit valve is filled with mustard!

- ### Bob's Lingerie and Skate Sharpening · Sault Ste. Marie, Ontario
  In hockey, skating is everything, and a poor skate sharpening will hurt your game. In the bedroom, the right lingerie has the ability to take any evening into "overtime." If undies and a sharpening are what you're after, Bob's in Sault Ste. Marie is a must. Not only is Bob a master at creating a precision edge on any blade, he is a genius when it comes to constructing a custom longline bra that's perfect under a sheer top or light sweater. Just make sure you're buying the right type of garters, because he does sell both.

- ### The App Store · Saskatoon, Saskatchewan
  The owners of this store were so inspired by smartphones and all the apps that could be purchased virtually that in 2011 they decided to open a real-life version. At this boutique, you can buy the actual equivalent of every app imaginable. The real-life camera app? It's a camera. The real-life Wikipedia app? It's a 26-volume encyclopedia. The real-life calendar app? It's a bunch of paper with squares on it.

- ### The Bunkbunkbed Barn · Thunder Bay, Ontario
  Most bed stores will only have one or two bunkbeds in stock. That's why it's so unusual to find a store that sells only bunkbeds. And if you thought *that* would be unusual, the Bunkbunkbed Barn will blow you away. This store only sells bunkbunkbeds—that's

bunkbeds with a third bunk on top. It's a must-see store, especially if you're a set of triplets with very high ceilings.

• **Woolco · Canada-wide**

With 160 locations nationwide, this full-service department store will provide you with an almost ideal shopping experience. If you're the type of shopper who appreciates taking a 5-cent ride on a coin-operated tiny pink elephant, this is your store. If you celebrate a near perfect day over a grilled cheese sandwich in a quiet in-store café tucked away behind the blouses and brassieres, this is your place. Woolco is the type of store that leaves you thinking, "It's not possible for a store this perfect to ever go out of business." Thankfully, we don't think it ever will.

Sizing

Shopping for clothes in Canada is a challenge because of the country's unorthodox sizing system. Here are a couple of examples.

MEN'S SHOES

UK	7	8	9	10	11
USA	7 ½	8 ½	9 ½	10 ½	11 ½
Europe	41	42	43	44 ½	46
Canada	Jennifer	Carla	Gwendolyn	Patricia ½	Claire

WOMEN'S CLOTHING

UK	8	10	12	14	16
USA	6	8	10	12	14
Europe	36	38	40	42	44
Canada	Lemon	Star	Smiley face	Diamond	14

- **Fab Grabbers · Canada-wide**

If Randy River and Suzy Shier made love at Le Chateau, their off-spring would be named Fab Grabbers. Attached to most Kernels franchises, this discount unisex clothier has locations in malls across the country. From denim vests to satin hip slips, Fab Grabbers has the perfect outfit for almost every Canadian occasion, including a formal bush party.

Architecture

While most of Canada contains characterless office buildings dating back to the 1960s and '70s, there is an abundance of faceless structures from the '80s, '90s, and 2000s as well. Prominent building materials in Canada include wood, stone, and pink insulation. In major cities, skylines have made way for breathtakingly straightforward condominiums (long for "condo") and a considerable number of big-box stores inspired by humanity's greatest invention, big boxes.

But landscape architecture is where Canadian ingenuity really soars. With so many natural materials to work with, many

Quebec's stunning Centre de Commerce

The Westerson House—what a beauty

parks in Canada appear as though no thought at all was put into designing them.

To learn more about Canada's notable architecture, visit Wikipedia. In the meantime, here are a few must-see architectural wonders.

• Westerson House · Alberta

Westerson House was designed by architect Terry Hubbard and completed in 1988. This marvel of construction stands as one of Hubbard's masterpieces, both for its vibrancy and for its integration with the natural surroundings. After completion, *Time* magazine called the home "perfect" and listed it as "one of the places you must see before you die." Now a national landmark, Westerson House is open to the public and easy to find. It's at the end of Oakwood Drive, down Lamplock Crescent. If you have the time, take a bounce on the original trampoline, which still stands in the backyard.

• Centre de Commerce · Quebec

A wonder of engineering and design at the time of construction, Centre de Commerce has come to represent human achievement the world over. Fighting the crowds to see this iconic seven-storey tower is worth it—especially to experience the thrilling elevator ride to the top. While up there, dine at the world's only square revolving restaurant, Lazy Susan's, where you can also buy a miniature model of the tower for $13.

• The Coquihalla Toll Booths · British Columbia

Located on Highway 5 in BC and spanning eight lanes, these toll booths are a testament to humankind's command of steel and concrete. Revolutionary in design, they were the first toll booths to incorporate a little hook to hang the toll booth operator's coat. If you're lucky enough, you may witness an 18-wheeler in its natural habitat, the weigh scale, during the annual migration to Vancouver.

Royal Horse Hotel · Alberta

Nestled in the picturesque Rocky Mountains is this beautiful five-star hotel for horses. Designed by Lord Everett MacArthur as a gift for his wife, an avid horse rider, this equine palace features amenities most horse hotels forget about: extra-large doorways, heavy-duty elevators, and industrial shampoo dispensers. Looking for a romantic gallop? Leave the kids at Fillies & Foals, the world's biggest horse waterpark!

The Paper House · Newfoundland

This rural house was built in the early 18th century in the Folio Gothic style of architecture. As its name suggests, it was built out of paper, and it did not survive its first winter. The family

TOP: The Paper House BOTTOM: The Commonwealth Bridge

that lived in it were so ashamed, they were forced to return to Ireland. Today, an exact replica of the Paper House stands in its place, made out of wood, stone, glass, and shingles. It remains worth a visit, if you like regular houses.

• The Commonwealth Bridge · Manitoba

The Commonwealth Bridge, completed in 2013, serves as a connector between Western Canada and Eastern Canada. Sitting atop *Bridge Monthly*'s list of "The 10 Most Beautiful Bridges in the World," the bridge has become a symbol of optimism, inspiring visitors to dream that anything is possible. To fully experience this bridge, it is suggested that you cross on foot. Average length of crossing, 45 seconds.

• Dick Windsor Park · Ontario

The genius of this park is in its amenities. Without the walkway, lamps, and benches, it's just a field. These elements invite you to interact with the majesty of this landscape, which is ever-evolving, as the city workers often forget to mow it. The Dick Windsor design has inspired thousands of parks in Canada, including Herb Patterson Park, Doris Fletcher Park, and Art Carr Field.

||||||||||||||||||||||||||||||||||||||||||||||||||||||||||||||||||||||||||||||||||||||||||||||||

TOP FIVE WALKS IN CANADA

To the Gas Station

Generally speaking about 10 minutes long, a walk to the gas station to pick up a bag of chips is the best way to explore Canada. During this walk you'll be accompanied by the din of a busy street and the smell of thawing doggy doo-doo from last winter. If you're lucky, you will be passed by a guy on a stolen bike.

Travel Tip

Canadians love love. More importantly, they love people who are on their honeymoon. ALWAYS tell your cab driver you are on your honeymoon (even if you're not)—he'll upgrade you to the front seat.

The Walk of Shame

Walking home the morning after a romantic tryst in the clothes you wore out the night before is considered one of the nation's most celebrated walks. To experience this, consider taking on a Canadian lover. A simple "How's it goin'?" is a good way of expressing romantic interest.

Walking It Off

To appreciate this walk, you need to injure yourself while having fun. Although you may be too old to participate in activities such as dodge ball, the Worm, or jumping off a homemade ramp, do them anyway. Fall hard, tearing your Achilles tendon. While you hop around in circles, onlookers will sympathetically encourage you to "walk it off." To impress your Canadian hosts, make sure you do.

The Way-Farther-Than-You-Thought Walk

Many walks in Canada are way farther than you think. Most walks give you the initial impression that they are about 25 minutes

long. When you hit the 45-minute mark, you know you're in for it. At this point it's customary to curse the fact that you said no to a ride. At the one-hour mark, you won't be able to think anything except "This walk is way farther than I thought."

A Nice Walk

You'll know you're on a nice walk if someone in your walking party gently sighs, "This is nice."

||||||||||||||||||||||||||||||||||||||||||||||||||||||||||||||||||||||||||||||

Food and Drink

Three things leap to mind when you think of Canadian cuisine: breakfast, lunch, and dinner. Defining an overarching style of food is a little hard to do, but perhaps the best way of describing it is kinda like a food court: there's a little bit of everything, both familiar and adventurous. Most of it you'll never try because you go straight for the chicken balls with that red sauce.

• Breakfast

When it comes to breakfast, Canadians are very superstitious. If food is not consumed in the form of a circle, that typically means you'll have bad luck the rest of the day. Which is why the most popular breakfast is a circular pastry with a smaller circle cut from the centre. Breakfast sandwiches with sausage and egg are presented in the shape of a circle, cereal is served in circular bowls, and bacon is cut into floppy, circular pucks. This concept is even present in the way coffee and tea are consumed, out of cups with a circular rim. You can expect to pay between $3 and $12 for breakfast, and must always pay with coins. Why? Think about what shape coins are.

• Lunch

Most cafés and restaurants serve a daily lunch special, or, as it is called in Canada, Stuffing Hour. Although some of these combinations may seem unusual, Stuffing Hour is when you'll find true Canadian food. Examples include salted cod chops, dipped buns, mashed hash and grouper, stuffed grapefruit, and boiled chicken loaf. If you're having trouble deciding what to eat, most Canadians carry around a Canada Food Guide and will be happy to let you borrow it.

- **Dinner**

  Dinner in Canada is traditionally served at 6 p.m. and is meant to be eaten while watching television. Most restaurants will provide you with a TV tray and user-friendly remote. Meals generally consist of two courses: a Hot Eat and a Cool Treat. Hot Eats commonly come in burger form, but it is not unusual to be served a bowl of fusion something or other. Cool Treats are presented either in a tube, on a stick, or à la mode.

Restaurants

When you want to eat, restaurants have got you covered, and this country has dozens of them. From family fare to romantic nights out and even some charming greasy spoons, the options are endless for Canada's hungry little tourists. Chomp chomp chomp your way through this next section to find out where to eat in Canada. Mmmmmm!

• Family Restaurants

One More Bite · Red Deer

If a loud and chaotic dining experience is what your family is looking for, One More Bite in Red Deer is the spot. The genius of this restaurant shows in the simplicity of the menu. Offering just three items—grilled cheese, mac 'n' cheese, and chicken fingers—One More Bite makes choosing what meal your kids will hardly touch easy. Adorned with never fully cleaned booths and sippy-cup-stained tables, the restaurant provides parents with a temporary sanctuary to reflect on how tired they are and to look forward to finally making it to Grandpa's house.

Peter Papadopoulos's Pancakes and Pop Shop · Canada-wide
Founded in 1968 by former professional hockey player Peter Papadopoulos, this restaurant primarily serves two of the most popular delicacies in Canada: pancakes and pop. With locations everywhere, it has become more than just a restaurant—it's a symbol of Canadian culture and cuisine. To avoid looking like a tourist, order their signature menu item, a triple stack of pancakes thrice dipped in Canadian pop. Locals call this a Triple Driple. If you are lucky enough visit during their "Fold the flapjack a lot to claim the jackpot" promotion, make sure to take part: you could win a 1998 Hyundai Santa Fe.

Donair Shave Club · Halifax
Whether you spell it "donair" or "doner," Halifax is Canada's capital for the Middle Eastern lamb sandwich. And everybody's favourite part is watching your server shave meat off the big vertical rotisserie. Something's a little different at this '50s-diner style donair restaurant: every table gets its own miniature rotisserie and little meat razor, so you can finally shave your own meat while rockin' out to the sounds of Buddy Holly. It's a donair dream come true, and kids love it too!

TESTIMONIAL
"I ate all kinds of crazy food while strolling the midway at the Stampede. Suffering from a horrible tummy ache while dressed like a cowboy is a memory I'll cherish forever."
LAWRENCE LAWRENCE, MANCHESTER

• Casual Restaurants

Truck · Vancouver

Vancouver finally has a restaurant that capitalizes on the city's food truck craze. Truck is a sit-down restaurant that replicates every detail of the food truck experience: waiting in line, greasy food served in cardboard containers, and the scent of exhaust fumes piped into the restaurant. Instead of tables and chairs, hunker down on the indoor curb that runs the length of the dining area.

Chainz · Canada-wide

Chainz is one of the most popular chain restaurants in Canada. Offering value and mediocrity in both food and atmosphere, Chainz is the perfect place to munch on some "appies" while involuntarily watching UFC on one of the 17 big-screen TVs. With restaurants conveniently located everywhere in Canada, this place perfectly fills the void when members of your party are "hangry" and can't decide where else to go. It's also the ideal place to watch your dad awkwardly flirt with a waitress as they both struggle to pronounce "ciabatta bread."

Sensory Overload · Edmonton

While movie theatres adopt 4-D immersive rumble seats to enhance the cinematic experience, this restaurant uses them to enhance the dining experience. These state-of-the-art seats use movement and stimuli to work in partnership with your meal. For example, ordering seafood? Hold on as your chair rocks like a ship on the waves while a small nozzle mists you with salt water. Wine and cheese? Feel the clatter of a bicycle on ancient French cobblestones while a small nozzle mists you with perfume. Salad? Feel the achingly slow push of vegetables emerging from dirt while a small nozzle mists you with dirt.

Ordering Food

Ordering food in Canada can be a little intimidating because, in addition to the standard courses (appetizer, entrée, and dessert), there may be up to 24 additional sub-courses. A meal might end up looking like this:

- Water
- Drinks
- Something a little naughty
- Pick-me-ups
- Whistle wetters
- Appetizers
- Nibbles
- Breadlers
- Tasty teasers

- Sharezies
- Nonstop pop
- Tapas
- Second chances
- Bits 'n' bites
- Salad knots
- Soupwiches
- Chowder
- New forks
- Entrées

- More water
- Meat
- Roasts
- Grillers
- Dessert
- Chillers
- Poofies
- Never-stop pop
- Coffee

- **Fine Dining**

Café Gary at the Four Seasons · Montreal

This swanky bistro made headlines recently for having a $10,000 hamburger on the menu. The burger is made up of coffee-rubbed Kobe beef, beluga caviar, Atlantic lobster, black truffles, edible gold leaf, and ninety-two $100 bills.

Le Chateau · Regina

Canada's premier clubwear retailer has just opened up its flagship restaurant in Regina's Midtown Mall. It's a playground of culinary ideas that reflect the fun, chic style of Le Chateau. Accessorize your salad with sparkly tomatoes and jangly croutons. The jewellery may be fake, but the flavours are real. Couples beware: There are very few offerings for men.

Bone Appetit · Calgary

The true food movement reaches its apex at this trendy all-bone gastropub. And yes, everything has a bone in it! Fine-dining staples get an orthopaedic twist, like bone-in ribeye with crunchy bone fritz, risotto with bone shavings, bone chops, and

The Vegetarian Code

Canada has only recently become friendly toward vegetarians and vegans. A few years ago, the only vegetarian options available at most restaurants were ketchup packets and moist towelettes. Now most restaurants have plenty of vegetarian options. Look for these symbols on most menus:

V = Vegetarian   **V** = Vegan   **V** = Venison

double-bone salmon. For dessert, try the marrow tiramisu (say that five times fast) or Jell-O.

• Interacting with Your Server

The server–eater relationship is a sacred one, its movements understated and beautiful, like a ballet. As the diner, your role is to lure your server in, send them away, and then lure them back. Send them away. Lure them back. Send them away. Lure them back. You may send them away by ordering food or asking for new cutlery. Lure them back with a wave or some simple eye contact.

The Red Light District

Amsterdam's infamous red light district is a carnival of salaciousness, with brothels, raucous bars, strip clubs, and haze-filled "coffee shops." Canada doesn't have one of these.

Servers may only return on their own if they use one of the following sentences:

"How are the first few bites?"

"So, what are we thinking?"

"Can I get you another pop?"

"My shift is ending, but Janet's gonna take care of you."

"I'll just get this out of your way."

"Can I tempt anyone with some dessert?"

"Here's your bill. No rush at all."

Tipping more than 10 percent is illegal in Canada, according to Canadian grandparents.

- **Alcohol**

Buying alcohol in many parts of the country is a frustrating and confusing endeavour. Which is why most Canadians choose to buy their booze at a dépanneur in Quebec, or from a guy named Ken. In restaurants, wine is available by the bottle or the glass. In bars, it is available only by the pitcher.

Beer is religion in Canada, and breweries are like churches. The big breweries are slowly being replaced by microbreweries, which will soon be replaced by nanobreweries—tiny breweries that are quickly built around you the moment you want a beer.

- **Non-alcoholic Drinks**

Pop.

IIIIIIIIIIIIIIIIIIIIIIIIIIIIIIIIIIIIIIIIIIIIIIIIIIIIIIIIIIIIIIIIIIIIIIIIIIIIIIIIIIIIIIIIIII
PLACES TO GO: PARKS AND GARDENS

• Stanley Park
The gem of Vancouver, this 1,000-acre park sits at the edge of downtown on the shore of the Pacific and is a gathering spot for everyone from nature lovers to nature toleraters. The park boasts the city's aquarium, a miniature railway, dozens of hiking trails, and seven parking spots.

Getting Around
Millions each year are drawn to the park's breathtaking seawall, a 9-kilometre paved route around the park with lanes for pedestrians, cyclists, and rollerbladers. While only one guy still rollerblades, the city doesn't have the heart to get rid of his lane.

First-time visitors, we recommend renting a tandem bike to explore the park while you argue with your partner, who isn't pedalling as hard as you.

What to Look Out For
Stanley Park is home to all kinds of wildlife, including coyotes, beavers, squirrels, and over 200 types of birds. While there are signs posted that prohibit feeding the animals, what are you, afraid of signs? We believe raccoons wouldn't survive without humankind's handouts of popcorn, chips, and that shawarma you couldn't finish. So remember to pack a little nibble for these bandits.

• Baffin Island Waterpark
Billed as the most difficult waterpark in the world to get to, Spashin' Island on Baffin Island, Nunavut, is a slide-

Did You Know
Stanley Park is home to half a million trees, although we're not sure—it might just be the same tree over and over.

chaser's dream. With 51 slides, 2 wave pools, 3 lazy rivers, and a surfing safari simulator, Splashin' Island offers something for everyone. People from all over the world make the arduous journey to experience extreme slides like the Caribou Crusher, which sends riders down a near vertical course straight into a spiral vortex. Or the Thundering Tundra, which zooms sliders down a pitch-black tube while gallons of water come thundering down behind. The Polar Pool lazy river perfectly simulates sitting on a block of ice that floats down a near frozen river.

Travel Tip

If you want to get up early to avoid the crowds, shower at night and sleep in the next day's clothes. You may also eat breakfast at dinnertime and brush your teeth two days ago.

What You Need to Know

Summer is very short on Baffin Island. For this reason, Splashin' Island is only open for five days at the beginning of August. The bugs on Baffin Island are horrendous; renting a full-body wetsuit and fencer's helmet is highly recommended.

• Maple Leaf Gardens

Maple Leaf Gardens has long been considered one of the original "cathedrals" of iced hockey. Former home to the Toronto Maple Leaves for over 65 years, this historic national shrine was finally converted into a Loblaws grocery store in 2011. No visit to Canada can be considered complete without stopping and shopping at the Maple Leaf Gardens Loblaws.

What to Do

Stroll the grocery aisles while soaking up Canada's rich iced hockey history within one of iced hockey's most beloved iced hockey houses. Score a "home run" with your guests by filling

A good time is had by all at the Baffin Island Waterpark

Historic Maple Leaf Gardens

your basket with some delicious President's Choice Meat Lasagna right where several iced hockey matches occurred. Peruse the exemplary cheese selection where puck met Cup in '67, or fight your way through the deli aisle where generations of punch onlookers whistled and hooted at their favourite punches. Don't forget to skim through the flyer for weekly specials.

What You Need to Know
- Store hours are from 7 a.m. to 11 p.m.
- Free parking with in-store purchase of $20 or more.
- There is no longer a fee for plastic bags.
- There is also an LCBO for those wanting to relive having a second-intermission brandy, or simply to drink and shop.

Music

"Music has the power to inspire Canadian musicians to pursue a career in the States." —Unknown Musician

Music is Canada's national pastime. All across the country—on frozen ponds, in arenas, and in suburban driveways—Canadians play music. The exact origins of music are unknown; however, we now recognize that the first ever song was played in Montreal in 1875. In the present day, the music of Canada assumes many styles and can be found on every corner.

• Canadian Rock 'n' Roll

Canadian rock 'n' roll emerged in the late 1950s with the arrival of groups like the Doug Dougs and Doug and the Doug Outs. Rootsy at first, Canadian rock 'n' roll has since evolved to a heavier sound. Most of what you'll hear today on rock radio sounds like a cross between Doug 'n' Dougers and the Doug Brothers Doug. It's good.

> **Pop Quiz**
>
> What do Neil Young, Justin Bieber, Joni Mitchell, Leonard Cohen, The Barenaked Ladies, Céline Dion, Paul Anka, Carly Rae Jepsen, k.d. lang, Drake, Shania Twain, Rush, Corey Hart, Anne Murray, and The Guess Who all have in common? They all played the recorder in grade 4 in Canada.

• Canadian Jazz

As one of the most respected Canadian art forms, jazz can be found almost everywhere in Canada. Spawning the musical careers of jazz greats like Quibley Flipper and Bessie Mable Ida Clarence, Canadian clubs primarily play jazz, and by law 60 percent of all Canadian songs must be played with a syncopated beat. If you're looking to hear the most authentic jazz in the country, check out Scuba-Dooba-Scapalapa-Doot-Squibly-Bops in Old Montreal. You will not be disappointed.

- **Canadian Classical Music**

Interest in Canadian classical music really took off in 1977 with the release of *Star Wars*. Children everywhere, wanting to emulate John Williams, begged their parents to buy them a cello. Thus began the rise of "Generation O" (for "orchestral"). It's not uncommon in urban Canada to witness impromptu string quartets gathered around a barrel fire, jammin' up a Mozart.

- **Canadian Country**

All Canadians have a country side—usually their mother's. It's a dominant gene which manifests itself any time Canadians get 20 minutes out of a major city. Canadian country legend Corn Westley once drunkenly said, "Canadian country is so important because Canada *is* a country, and so are we all, aren't we?"

- **Canadian Folk**

From the Celtic songs of the Maritimes to more contemporary tunes, folk music has been a part of Canada for as long as brooding young men have been bringing acoustic guitars to parties and singing unprompted. Popular themes in Canadian folk music include the water, the wheat, the rock, the sky, the woods, the wonder, the city, the light, the love, and girls. If you want to make it in Canadian folk music, apparently you should head to the rootsy folk clubs of Yorkville in downtown Toronto.

- ### Canadian Rap
Toronto is Canada's hip-hop hub, homies, and it's the birthplace of Canada's greatest rapper, Cory Raps-a-Bunch, who you may remember from 2016's song of the summer, "Let's Everybody Be Calm on the Bus, Okay?" Canadian rap is distinct from its American counterparts in many ways, most notably in its use of cuss-free language, its references to practical automobiles, and its frequent samples of the Doug Brothers Doug.

- ### Canadian EDM
Canada has had electronic music since the country first got electricity, in 1987. Popular DJs include #hashtag, 3arg4sm, Flippy Flopp, and Tie Domi.

Radio

The Canadian government requires all radio stations to be named after wild animals.

- The Eagle: Hits of the '80s
- The Fox: '70s Soft Rock
- The Bear: Hits of the '50s, '60s, and '80s, but not the '70s
- The Rat: Alt Rock of March 1997 through September 2000
- The Wolf: Golden Oldies and Doobie Newbies
- The Deer: Rural Urban
- The Bull: Country
- The Otter: Jazz Country
- The Crow: Sports Talk Radio by hosts wearing sunglasses
- The Moose: Mark Messier Radio

Live Music

Planning to see a concert at a club? If the ticket says 8:00 p.m., that's not when the music starts. The concert will likely unfold as follows:

8:00	Doors open		1:15	Unnecessary encore
9:00	DJ set		1:45	Are-you-kidding-me encore
10:00	Opening band		2:00	Club closes
10:45	Second opening band		3:30	After-hours encore
11:30	Headline band		5:00	Sleepytime encore
12:00	Predictable encore		7:00	Band continues to play for par-
12:45	Second encore			ticipants in a fun run outside

Singing the National Anthem

Before sporting events, it is customary to remove your hat during the national anthem, "O Canada." If you did not bring a hat, one will be provided for you to remove. To fit in with the Canadian crowd, always sing the first line of the anthem with gusto and then kinda half mutter and talk-sing the rest.

Spectator Sports

Dog racing is the most popular summer sport in Canada, with every major city having its own track and holding weekly events. This all culminates with the Grand Hound, a national tournament of 16 dogs that is covered for weeks in the national press. You might not want to attend if you're uncomfortable with public displays of affection, as the crowd at the dog track is mostly made up of teenagers who have come to make out.

Many summer festivals also feature traditional Canadian sports, such as rock throwing, torso grappling, the climb, hick-and-huck (a twine-and-ball game), curse hurling, and la saute (a Manitoban jump dance).

Also during the summer, lake communities are invaded by rowdy fanatics of the country's unofficial summer sport, jet-skiing. Riders perform graceful dance routines atop gnarly Sea-Doos as throngs of hooligans slam energy drinks and chant along to the accompanying classical music. Riders compete in men's, women's, and pairs (the most dangerous sport in the world).

While winter sports do exist in Canada, they are unpopular.

• Golf

Canada is a golfer's paradise, with thousands of world-class courses. The options are endless. If you need help choosing which course to play, use the table below. Pick one name from the first column, another from the second column, and one from the third. Then look them up and book a round.

Stony	Meadows	Golf and Country Club
Rocky	Creek	Golf and Country Club
Pine	Quest	Golf and Country Club
Oak	Pond	Golf and Country Club
Emerald	Hills	Golf and Country Club
Falcon	Sands	Golf and Country Club
Championship	Grove	Golf and Country Club
Lonesome	Brook	Golf and Country Club
Harvest	Glen	Golf and Country Club
Willow	View	Golf and Country Club
Eagle	Springs	Golf and Country Club
Silver	Park	Golf and Country Club
Valley	Ridge	Golf and Country Club
Ridge	Valley	Golf and Country Club
Heather	Hollow	Golf and Country Club
Busty	Lake	Golf and Country Club
Chunky	Beaches	Golf and Country Club
Chesty	Wood	Golf and Country Club
Bethany	Canyon	Golf and Country Club
Seymour	Gardens	Golf and Country Club

The World's Biggest Ringette Stick

The Kindersley Community Centre, Saskatchewan, is proud to be the home of the largest ringette stick in the world: 200 feet long, and weighing a staggering 50,000 pounds. It was, however, originally supposed to be a hockey stick. There is some debate as to whether the town ran out of money or the artist got lazy, but needless to say, this shaft is bladeless and ready to impress.

Unfortunately, the arena structure itself was unable to support the weight of the stick, which therefore lies horizontal in the parking lot, leaving many to wonder if it is just a downed hydro pole.

Holidays

When travelling, it is important to make note of Canadian holidays. During these times nothing really changes, except liquor stores close and junk-mail delivery stops.

• No Family Day

No Family Day is a statutory holiday observed by many regions to encourage Canadians who identify as "single" or "without family" to live free from the judgment of society. On this day (July 8th), singles get exclusive access to places they normally feel excluded from, such as family restaurants, the science centre, and bowling alleys.

Fun Fact

The phrase "Table for one" is muttered 1.2 million times on No Family Day.

• Doctor Day

It's common knowledge that Canada has universal health care. But did you know that the law requires every citizen to visit the doctor for a checkup on the exact same day? To ensure a healthy nation, every Canadian spends all of April 30th waiting in line outside a local school for their chance to stick out their tongue and say "awww." If this sounds like a serious occasion, it's not. A tailgate-like atmosphere usually spreads throughout the crowd, and it's not uncommon for everyone, including the doctors, to be slightly intoxicated.

NOTE: Do not expect to get surgery on Doctor's Day. Surgery Day is a completely different holiday.

• Reading Week

Not to be confused with the many reading weeks that occur at postsecondary institutions, *this* Reading Week is a week-long holiday that forces Canadians to read Canadian literature. Each

Canadians waiting to see the doctor on Doctor Day

citizen must complete at least three novels written by either Margaret Atwood, Michael Ondaatje, Margaret Atwood, or Michael Ondaatje. The book you are currently reading would most certainly not qualify as a Reading Week book. Actually reading it during that time might even be a criminal offence.

- **Smitty's Day**

The first Tuesday in February is a celebration of Canada's most popular nickname, Smitty. If you go by that moniker, you are set for the day. People nicknamed Smitty can take the day off work, eat free meals at any restaurant in the country, then get free admission to the annual Smitty Awards. This is the media event of the year, where people nicknamed Smitty are honoured with trophies to recognize their achievements as well as their friendly demeanour. The day also causes envy and resentment in people with Canada's second most popular nickname, Murph.

- **Gentle Day**

Toddlers are well known for their unchecked exuberance. They devote 100 percent of their effort to every single activity, whether it's closing a door, kicking an airplane seat, or pulling a dog's tail. After Canadian parents grew tired of yelling "Gentle!," the government decided to make last Sunday in July "Gentle Day." On this day, cars cannot be driven above 5 kilometres an hour and all citizens must use inside voices.

- **Santa Claus's Birthday**

Everybody loves Santa Claus, but in Canada they actually celebrate the jolly old elf's birthday. And it's not December 25th—it's *April* 11th. On this day, Canadians celebrate by participating in Santa's favourite activity: going to Mexico for a week.

- **Hallontine's Day**

June 23rd is the halfway point between Valentine's Day and Halloween, and on this day, Canadians combine the two holidays in a wild celebration of love and death. Revellers go door to door to make out with strangers, children compose love letters to ghosts on Ouija boards, and Canadians everywhere explore their deep, dark fears of intimacy. Also, there's both kinds of candy: little chocolate bars and cinnamon hearts.

TESTIMONIAL
"Almost too friendly, I'd say."
KLAUS, GERMANY

- **Ford Employee Pricing Days**

From late July to early August, Canadians can save over $10,000 on a Ford F150 XLT 4x4 SuperCab. Through dealer incentives and rebates, Canadians average a savings of about $3,900 off the MSRP of all Ford models, from the sporty Mustang to the economical Fusion. That makes this the right time to get into a Ford!

IIIIIIIIIIIIIIIIIIIIIIIIIIIIIIIIIIIIIIIIIIIIIIIIIIIIIIIIIIIIIIIIIIIIIIIIIIIIIIIIIIIIIIIIIII
PLACES TO GO: CANADIAN WONDERS

• Niagara Falls

Known for its romantic views and one-of-a-kind scenery, this iconic and monumental natural wonder has earned a score of 4.4 on Yelp. And it truly is a marvel. In fact, in the time it takes you to read this sentence, over six seconds' worth of water will have spilled over the Falls. That's a lotta bathtubs!

In addition to being the Honeymoon Capital of the World, Niagara Falls is also known as the Blue Plastic Poncho Capital of the World, the Coin-Operated Binoculars Capital of the World, and the White Noise Machine Capital of the World.

Speak Up

The constant noise (probably over 500 decibels, if that means anything to you) generated by the Falls makes it nearly impossible for tourists to carry on a conversation. Because of this, Niagara has become a go-to destination for people who want to confess to any number of sins or crimes. Want to tell your parents what really happened to their vase? Tell them at the Falls. They'll never hear you, but your conscience will be clear.

More Fun than a Barrel of You!

When you first set eyes on Niagara Falls, you may be tempted to get in and ride over the edge in a wooden barrel. That would be foolish, because you're going to pay tourist prices for any barrel you buy in town. Instead, go two towns over and buy a barrel from the local cooper, Mr. Cooper.

Did You Know

If you stretched a shower curtain from one end of the Falls to the other, it would cost almost $400!

• The Bay of Fundy

Home to the highest tides in the world, the Bay of Fundy was, in 2009, diagnosed by the World Oceanographers Association as clinically insane. Twice every single day, 100 billion tons of water rise and fall 55 feet, causing observers to hoot and holler as though they were at a rock concert. It is not uncommon to hear onlookers chant, "TIDE PRIDE! TIDE PRIDE! TIDE PRIDE!" until it has fully gone out, which usually takes about six hours. At low tide this psychotic bay can be explored by walking on the ocean floor. At high tide you can stand on the shore and just kinda look at what appears to be the normal ocean.

Lunch at Washaways

Every day the dedicated staff at Washaways rebuilds their beloved restaurant on the ocean floor of Fundy from scratch. If

you are lucky enough to get a reservation during the three-hour period when the restaurant is not submerged, this is a dining experience you will not soon forget. After sucking back some buttery lobster, make your way back upshore to watch everything, from the table linens to the espresso machine, vanish and return back to the sea from whence they came. To cover the restaurant's operating costs, be prepared to pay $300 for an entree. That's the price to pay for eating at a temporary restaurant.

Kayak Attack

If you ask anyone who runs a sea kayaking outfit, they will tell you that renting a sea kayak is absolutely the best way of exploring the magnificent rock formations and sea-carved caves of Fundy. Be warned, however: You will want to journal this

Northern lights turned on

experience, and the more times you write "kayak" or "Fundy," the weirder the words look. Kayak, kayak, kayak, Fundy kayak, Fundy, kayak kayak kayak Fundy Fundy. You see?

- **Northern Lights**
No trip to Canada is complete without experiencing the impressive Northern Lights. More formally referred to as the "aurora borealis," these colourful dancing lights in the northern night sky put on quite the show for the thrilled onlookers below. When the Canadian Government turns the Northern Lights to the "on" position, they can be seen from many parts of Canada. The schedule for when the lights are turned "on" is constantly changing and often kept secret. Given the hourly operating cost of over $720,000, it is the sole digression of Canada's National Minister

of Illumination to pick and choose impactful times to power up the lights. It is a well-documented fact that if the Northern Lights were accidentally left "on" all the time, Canada's deficit would double in less than one calendar month. So count yourself fortunate if you happen to be visiting when the Minister flips the switch, and prepare yourself for what will undoubtedly be a very impressive show. Not Cirque du Soleil impressive, but then again, what is?

Looky Where?
Oftentimes visitors to Canada wonder, where's the best place to view the Northern Lights? The answer is obvious: from underneath the glass dome observation deck of a megayacht moored in the Northwest Passage. But that may not work for everyone's travel budget. Therefore, the next logical choice is Yellowknife. Known as the Las Vegas of the North (minus the buffets), Yellowknife is the definitive Northern Lights experience destination. From downtown sidewalks lined with large throw pillows, blankets, and binoculars to a municipal bylaw mandating a citywide "lights out" at 10 p.m., Yellowknife works hard to afford sky gazers the perfect pitch-black setting to fully observe the night sky while still offering the convenience of a nearby Quiznos.

App-tastic

If you've ever used Airbnb or Uber, you participated in what's known as the "sharing economy"—an economic model in which individuals are able to borrow or rent assets owned by someone else. In Canada, one of the most popular "sharing apps" is called MEAT ME. This app allows strangers to share, rent, or sell meat and poultry. So if you're travelling with unwanted sausages, MEAT ME makes it easy to find someone with a pork chop who's willing to trade.

Safety First

A couple of things to bear in mind: First, be careful when walking the streets of Yellowknife. Most people have their eyes permanently locked upward. Yellowknife leads the nation in pedestrian-on-pedestrian fatalities. These horrific accidents occur when two very excited Northern Light enthusiasts fatally collide while they are both fully running. Second, a visit to Yellowknife does not guarantee that you will see the Northern Lights. Again, that is solely at the digression of the government. But don't fear: with the legalization of marijuana, you can simply smoke some Master Bubba Kush at the Super 8 in Yellowknife and create an aurora experience of your own.

Travel Tip

Let your heart be your map. Or better yet, use a smartphone.

||||||||||||||||||||||||||||||||||||||||||||||||||||||||||||||||||||||||||||||||||

Index

About This is That

CBC Radio One's award-winning satirical program *This is That* is created by veteran comedians Pat Kelly and Peter Oldring, and produced by Chris Kelly, who use the familiar sound of public radio as a platform for character bits and improvisational comedy. The CBC radio show has engaged audiences across the country and beyond with an acclaimed radio show, podcast, and viral digital content. *This is That* stories have been covered by *Wall Street Journal, Boing Boing, Paste Magazine, New York Magazine, The Guardian, Devour*, and more. *This is That*'s live show tour has played to sold-out audiences; it will tour back across the country in January and February 2017. Learn more at:

www.cbc.ca/radio/thisisthat

www.cbc.ca/radio/podcasts/comedy/this-is-that/

Facebook · Twitter · Instagram: @CBCThisIsThat

This is That: Travel Guide to Canada was written by
Pat Kelly, Dave Shumka, Peter Oldring, and Chris Kelly.